I0625301

Mystery Babylon

U N V E I L E D

Lucifer the Queen of Heaven

Isaac Isaiah

Mystery Babylon Unveiled: Lucifer the Queen of Heaven
© Copyright 2023 by Isaac Isaiah - All rights reserved.
Published by Star of Elyon.
Detroit, Michigan.

Editor: Bryan Davidson
Cover illustration: Eldar Akmanaev

It is not legal to reproduce, duplicate, or transmit any part of this document in either electronic means or printed format. Recording of this publication is strictly prohibited.

The use of images in this book is protected under the FAIR USE Act. Under section 107 of the Copyright Act 1976, allowance is made for "fair use" for purposes such as criticism, commentary, news reporting, teaching, scholarship, education and research. Fair use is a use permitted by copyright statute that might otherwise be infringing.

CONTENTS

Figure 0-0-1: An advertisement for General Electricity Company Society (1892), depicting the Queen of Heaven bringing illumination and spiritual power.

INTRODUCTION

The identity of "MYSTERY, Babylon the Great" has been debated for ages. There is undoubtedly a city on earth that meets some of the conditions to fulfill the prophecy in Revelation chapter 17 but ultimately the prophecy is fulfilled in the spiritual realm. There is a terrestrial manifestation and there is a celestial manifestation. To suggest that there is a SPIRIT of Babylon is almost heresy to many Bible scholars, but it absolutely is real. Even more controversial is the suggestion of **who** that spiritual Babylon is. *Mystery Babylon Unveiled: Lucifer, the Queen of Heaven* will prove to you, with an abundance of biblical evidence, that the spiritual fulfillment of MYSTERY, Babylon is the very same spirit who is called Lucifer and Satan.

This book will also bring clarity to why such importance is placed on Babylon's judgement in the book of Revelation. Why is it that Babylon has three chapters dedicated to her indictment, her judgement, and the reaction of the saints to her judgement, while the Dragon and the Serpent get far less emphasis placed on events occurring with them? Why is it that the reverence for the Virgin Mary worldwide rivals the reverence for Jesus Christ? Why are nearly all cathedrals dedicated to "Our Lady"?

Where is Lucifer being worshiped like the Most High? Shouldn't we expect to see his goals manifested in our world? Read this book and you will understand that Lucifer is not a "he," but a SHE (and always has been). You will understand that every one of the "I will" statements made by Lucifer in Isaiah 14 has been fulfilled by the Virgin Mary, the Christianized version of the Queen of Heaven. You know that the woman riding the beast is called the Mother of Harlots, but did you know that this was a title also carried by a goddess? As will be proven in this book, the Queen of Heaven was called the Mother of the Gods; false gods in the Bible are called ABOMINATIONS. That makes her the Mother of Abominations! Another bullseye when identifying and exposing MYSTERY, Babylon!

Open goddess worship is increasing, and people are taking notice, but very few of them understand WHY it's happening. Often, what Christian authors do is gloss over information about goddesses because they are focused on everything masculine (which they believe the Devil to be); so, it falls to me bring forth the nuggets of truth that were overlooked. Using the Bible as my authority when it comes to discerning truth in all the material I've researched, I will put the pieces of the puzzle together and reveal the secret identity of the adversary who is called Satan and Lucifer to be the Great Whore of Babylon.

Even if you do not come to the same conclusion that I have by the end of this book, I am positive that you will still be enriched by the knowledge contained within. This book will sharpen your discernment and make sense of the goddess worship that this world is steeped in. I give all praise, all honor, and all glory to my Father YAHAWAH in Heaven (the God of Abraham, Isaac and Jacob), in the name of His only begotten son, Yahawashai, whom the world knows as Jesus the Christ.

Figure 1-0-1: A Babylonian relief of a goddess (possibly Inanna) standing on lions and flanked by owls.

CHAPTER 01: THIS IS WICKEDNESS

One of the reasons that Mystery Babylon has never been exposed as a spirit is the prevailing belief among believers of the Bible that there are no female spirits or female angels. This is not something that the Bible has indicated at all. The truth is that female spirits are in the Bible, and I will show you where this can be found.

Perhaps one of the most overlooked passages in the Bible is Zechariah 5:5-11. Even to distinguished Biblical scholars, these verses have proven difficult to adequately interpret. I have a very simple approach to it; that is to take it literally. Things often make perfect sense when you stop trying to make something that isn't a metaphor into a metaphor. As the passage reads:

> "Then the angel that talked with me went forth, and said unto me, Lift up now thine eyes, and see what is this that goeth forth. And I said, What is it? And he said, This is an ephah that goeth forth. He said moreover, This is their resemblance through all the earth. And, behold, there was lifted up a talent of lead: and **this is a woman** that sitteth in the midst of the ephah. And he said, **This is wickedness**. And he cast [the woman] into the midst of the ephah; and he cast the weight of lead upon the mouth thereof.
>
> Then lifted I up mine eyes, and looked, and, behold, there came out two women, and the wind was in their wings; for they had wings like the wings of a stork: and they lifted up the ephah between the earth and the heaven. Then said I to the angel that talked with me, Whither do these bear the ephah? And he said unto me, To build it an house in the land of Shinar: and it shall be established, and set there upon her own base." (Zechariah 5:5-11)

Here, we have three very interesting women who appear in the Bible. We know from the details given by Zechariah that at least two of these women have wings. Winged creatures in the Bible are typically spirits. Those two women lift the ephah (basket) and carry that basket off to the land of Shinar, the ancient location of Babylon, so that its contents can be placed on a pedestal in a house built for it. If these were two men, I doubt anyone would hesitate to call them angels. But since they are women, the tendency is to try to explain them away as symbols. It is important to note that with regard to Biblical prophecy, when a vision is symbolic it will be followed by an explanation of the meaning. The angel talking with Zechariah doesn't explain what these women represent. This means that these women are exactly what Zechariah sees—literal women with wings.

Furthermore, the description of these women does not involve similes (except as it relates to their wings). For example, the angel talking with Zechariah doesn't say that these women are *"as a"* or *"like a"* woman, he says that they **ARE** women. The only time he uses a simile is when he says that their wings are *"like"* the wings of a stork. There is nothing said or shown in this vision to lead us to the conclusion that these women are anything other than literal women.

Not that the existence of the two women with wings (dare I even say angels) isn't important by itself, but there is an even more important woman seen in Zechariah's vision. The woman who is being carried in that basket has two important titles given to her; the one that I will discuss first is "**WICKEDNESS**." No description is given of her, nor are any similes used, making it almost impossible to explain her away as a symbol for something else. Additionally, the angel talking with Zechariah does not give any symbolic meaning whatsoever with regard to her. I see no reason that she shouldn't be taken as the literal embodiment of Wickedness.

Again, I must emphasize that the angel speaking with Zechariah does not say that the subject is only appearing *"as"* or *"like"* a woman. There isn't any room—given the definitive language that is used—for us to draw the conclusion that her being a woman is a disguise. Neither this woman carried in the basket nor the woman riding the beast (Revelation 17) would be called a "woman" if it was a disguise. All scripture *is* given by inspiration of God (2 Timothy 3:16). If we insist that it is a disguise of Satan, despite this clear evidence in the scriptures before us, we would surely be suffering from a case of cognitive dissonance.

Some will bring up 2 Corinthians 11:14, which says, "And no marvel; for Satan himself is transformed into an angel of light." But how does transforming into an angel of light serve as proof that Satan is disguised as a woman? Let's read the verse and keep it in its proper context to understand what is really being said:

"For such are false apostles, deceitful workers, transforming themselves into the apostles of Christ. And no marvel; for Satan himself is transformed **into an angel of light**. Therefore it is no great thing if <u>his ministers also be transformed as **the ministers of righteousness;**</u> whose end shall be according to their works." (2 Corinthians 11:13-15)

The context is "deceitful workers" transforming themselves into "ministers of righteousness." The apostle Paul wasn't talking about changing genders. Satan is transformed into an angel of "**light**" and her ministers "**also**" are transformed into ministers of righteousness. Some may insist that Lucifer must use the disguise of a woman to deceive man. But let's keep this in mind: John 1:18 says, "No man hath seen God at any time…" and Jesus Christ says, in Matthew 18:10, "…in heaven their angels do always behold the face of my Father which is in heaven." To me, it's just plain ridiculous to suggest that Satan, who led a third of the angels who have beheld the face of God to rebel against Him, would need to use a female disguise to convince man to rebel against the same God **who he has never seen** at any time. It's a poorly thought-out justification for the belief that Satan is only disguised as a woman. I implore the reader, in love, to set aside their bias as we move forward in exposing the true identity of Lucifer.

The angel talking with Zechariah gives the woman who is called Wickedness a second identifier: the EYE. We will come back to this identifier later when we discuss symbols associated with Lucifer. What happens with this woman called wickedness is she is sealed (or hidden) underneath a lid and she is carried to the land of Shinar (Babylon). In Revelation 17, we see another woman who is wicked and lives in Babylon; a woman whose sins have "reached unto heaven". She rides on top of a scarlet-colored beast and has a name written on her forehead: **MYSTERY**, BABYLON THE GREAT, THE MOTHER OF HARLOTS AND ABOMINATIONS OF THE EARTH. This is most definitely the same woman from Zechariah 5. But here is the question: Revelation 17:18 says that the woman who John sees is "that great **city** which reigns over the kings of the earth," so how can it be true that she is the Devil?

Once you realize the connection that the city of Babylon has to the Queen of Heaven, it becomes clear that this is a prophecy that has two subjects; there is a Babylon in the natural realm and there is a Babylon in the spiritual realm. The Babylon in the spiritual realm is Lucifer. We have a rule for this in Ephesians 6:12, which says, "For we wrestle not against flesh and blood, but against principalities, against powers, against the rulers of the darkness of this world, against **spiritual wickedness** in high places." The prophecies against Babylon the Great are ultimately fulfilled in the spiritual realm and we will fully expose that spirit in this book.

Figure 1-0-1: The Caduceus Sculpture by James Muir invokes the image of the goddess Ishtar.

CHAPTER 02: LOST IN TRANSLATION

A major roadblock for many who hear me say that the Devil is a woman is the fact that the Bible calls the Devil, Satan, and the Dragon by the pronouns "he" and "him." That is due to something called grammatical gender. This isn't something that English speaking people are commonly aware of, but languages such as Hebrew and Greek have gender class assigned to nouns. When translating these languages to English, the gender class of nouns determine the gender of the pronoun that is used.

For example: in Psalm 34:2, King David refers to his soul as a "her." It reads: "My soul shall make **her** boast in the LORD: the humble shall hear thereof, and be glad."

This has led to some people saying that our spirits have a feminine characteristic, but that's not true. The word for soul in Hebrew is na'phash. Its gender class is feminine. Therefore, when translated to English, the pronoun added must be feminine as well, although David is a male. The words dragon, devil, serpent, and satan are all masculine class nouns. So, when they are translated to English, they must all be translated with masculine pronouns attached to them.

Looking at Isaiah 14's prophecy about Lucifer, let's acknowledge what should be obvious to everyone: there are TWO subjects being addressed in this prophecy. In Isaiah chapter 14, verses 12 through 15, the Most High calls the earthly king (Nebuchadnezzar) by the name Lucifer, comparing him to the star Venus. So, you have a subject in the terrestrial and you have a subject in the celestial, a subject in the material world and a subject in the spiritual world.

Because this prophecy is directed against a man on the earth first, it shouldn't be considered odd that he is called the "son of the morning." With that being said, the word BENE (Strong's H1121), which is translated as "son," can also mean "child." English speakers assume the word "son" in the phrase *"son of the morning,"* just like as in *"sons of God,"* can only mean a male offspring. What should we do with 1 John 3:2 in that case? That says, "Beloved, now are we the **sons** of God..." (1 John 3:2)

Should we exclude women here because the verse uses the word "sons"? Or should we understand that we're dealing with a figure of speech, and that women are included under the term *"sons of God?"* It's clearly a figure of speech. We have a prophecy in Isaiah 14 where one subject is a king on earth, and the other subject is the star Venus in the heavens.

Another issue that comes up, and this is more of a problem of interpretation, is the incorrect teaching about gender in the afterlife (or in the resurrection). It comes from a misinterpretation of what Jesus Christ said about angels when he was asked who a woman's husband will be if she was widowed seven times.

In Matthew 22:30, Jesus says of people who have died in the faith, "For in the resurrection they neither marry, nor are given in marriage, but are as the angels of God in heaven." Although he never said anything about being genderless or being androgynous, people have formed that interpretation and run with it. This is due to Gnostic influence, and the mingling in of their doctrines about the spirit world being a place of "oneness" where there are no true divisions, even among genders. But the God of the Bible is a SEPARATOR. He separates the opposites. The correct interpretation of what Jesus Christ said about angels can be understood just from reading the same answer in Luke:

"And Jesus answering said unto them, The children of this world marry, and are given in marriage: But they which shall be accounted worthy to obtain that world, and the resurrection from the dead, neither marry, nor are given in marriage: **Neither can they die any more**: for they are **equal** unto the angels..." (Luke 20:34-36)

Because they cannot die anymore—that's how humans will be like the angels. YAH is not a God who mixes the opposites. He is not a gender-bender, nor does he create gender-benders. He made male and female and said that any confusion of the two is an abomination to him (Deuteronomy 22:5). Isn't it true that our Father in Heaven is a HE? God has made it clear that He is not a "THEY" or an "IT." If you believe spirits can change genders, or that they don't have genders at all, then how doesn't that include our FATHER in Heaven too? As further support that there is a divide between male and female in the spiritual realm, I would like to draw your attention to the creation of man in Genesis.

"And God said, Let us make man in our image, after our likeness: and let them have dominion over the fish of the sea, and over the fowl of the air, and over the cattle, and over all the earth, and over every creeping thing that creepeth upon the earth. So God created man in his own image, in the image of God created he him; **male and female created he them**." (Genesis 1:26-27)

The word for "him" and "man" is ADAM (Strong's H120), as in mankind. The word translated as "image" is SELEM (Strong's H6754); it is defined as "image, likeness (of resemblance)." The word translated as "likeness" is DAMUT (Strong's H1823) and is defined as "likeness, similitude, of external appearance." In Genesis

5:2, the Bible says that God "called their name Adam, in the day when they were created" in His image. Jesus Christ says in Mark 10:6, "But from the beginning of the creation God made them **male and female**." Those are the images (or patterns) of bodies in both heaven and on earth. God did not create androgynous beings.

The language of Hebrew, created by YAH almighty, has masculine and feminine words. It should not be a surprise to us that we find women with wings in the book of Zechariah. If there are angels who look like men, why wouldn't there also be angels (or spirits) who look like women?

Figure 2-0-1: "The Birth of Venus" by Sandro Botticelli.

Figure 2-0-2: An image of the Spirit of Freemasonry, from the book, Freemasonry, by W. Kirk MacNulty.

CHAPTER 03: YOUR FATHER THE DEVIL

A question that is surely on everyone's mind is: if Lucifer is a woman, why does Jesus say that the Devil is the "father" of liars? The answer to this question can be found in the Scriptures. In John 8:37-41, Jesus Christ was talking to Judeans, some of whom did not believe on him. To them he proclaimed:

"I know that ye are Abraham's seed; but ye seek to kill me, because my word hath no place in you. I speak that which I have seen with my Father: and ye do that which ye have seen with your father. They answered and said unto him, Abraham is our father. Jesus saith unto them, If ye were Abraham's children, ye would do the works of Abraham. **But now ye seek to kill me, a man that hath told you the truth**, which I have heard of God: this did not Abraham. Ye do the deeds of your father." (John 8:37-41)

There is a comparison to what happened between Cain and Abel being made by Jesus Christ here. The Judeans sought to kill Jesus, just as Cain slew his righteous brother Abel because his own deeds were evil. As Jesus said to the Judeans, "now ye seek to kill me, a man that has told you the truth." As the passage continues, we find that Jesus Christ identified exactly who their "father" was by telling us more about what his deeds were. As we read in verses 41 through 44:

"Then said they to him, We be not born of fornication; we have one Father, even God. Jesus said unto them, If God were your Father, ye would love me: for I proceeded forth and came from God; neither came I of myself, but he sent me. Why do ye not understand my speech? even because ye cannot hear my word. Ye are of your father the devil, and the lusts of your father ye will do. **He was a murderer from the beginning, and abode not in the truth**, because there is no truth in him. When he speaketh a lie, he speaketh of his own: for he is a liar, and the father of [liars]." (John 8:37-44)

The "devil" that Jesus Christ was speaking about was a murderer from the beginning and he abode not in the truth. We can go to the beginning (Genesis) and read about him, and we'll see when and how he did not abide in "the truth". Reading Genesis chapter 4:3-7:

"And in process of time it came to pass, that Cain brought of the fruit of the ground an offering unto the LORD. And Abel, he also brought of the firstlings of his flock and of the fat thereof. And the LORD had respect unto Abel and to his offering: But unto Cain and to his offering he had not respect. And Cain was very wroth, and his countenance fell. And the LORD said unto Cain, Why art thou wroth? and why is thy countenance fallen? **If thou doest well, shalt thou not be accepted?** and if thou doest not well, sin lieth at the door. And unto thee shall be his desire, and thou shalt rule over him." (Genesis 4:3-7)

In this passage the Creator tells Cain that if he does well, he will be accepted. This indicates that there was **a truth** that Cain knew which he should have been abiding by. What was that truth? There are several scriptures that provide the answer. 1 John 2:4 reads, "He that saith, I know him, and <u>keepeth not his commandments</u>, is a liar, and **the truth** is not in him." Simply put, the "truth" is God's commandments. The commandments have always been with man, even before Mt. Sinai, as evidenced by the Creator telling Cain that he would accept him if he did well. We can sum up the commandments, or THE TRUTH, very simply in Mark 12:29-33:

"And Jesus answered him, The first of all <u>the commandments</u> is, Hear, O Israel; The Lord our God is one Lord: And thou shalt love the Lord thy God with all thy heart, and with all thy soul, and with all thy mind, and with all thy strength: this is the first commandment. And the second is like, namely this, Thou shalt love thy neighbour as thyself. There is none other commandment greater than these. And the scribe said unto him, Well, Master, thou hast said **the truth**: for there is one God; and there is none other but he: And to love him with all the heart, and with all the understanding, and with all the soul, and with all the strength, <u>and to love his neighbour as himself, is more than all whole burnt offerings and sacrifices.</u>" (Mark 12:29-33)

This is **THE TRUTH** that Cain did not abide in. This truth was not given by Yah to any of the angels; the commandments were only given to man. Rather than abiding in the truth that was given to him straight from the mouth of God, he sought to kill his righteous brother because his own deeds were evil. We see this in Genesis 4:8-9:

"And Cain talked with Abel his brother: and it came to pass, when they were in the field, that Cain rose up against Abel his brother, **and slew him**. And the LORD said unto Cain, Where is Abel thy brother? And he said, **I know not: Am I my brother's keeper**?" (Genesis 4:8-9)

Not only did Cain kill his own brother but he then lied, straight to the face of God, about not knowing where his brother was. If Cain had possessed the love that he was supposed to have in his heart, he would have been his brother's keeper. As Jesus Christ said, THESE ARE NOT THE DEEDS OF ABRAHAM. In Matthew 23:34-35, Jesus names Abel as the first person whose blood was shed upon the earth. By doing this, Jesus is also comparing those responsible for the deaths of the righteous to Cain. The passage reads:

"Wherefore, behold, I send unto you prophets, and wise men, and scribes: and some of them ye shall kill and crucify; and some of them shall ye scourge in your synagogues, and persecute them from city to city: That upon you may come all the righteous blood shed upon the earth, **from the blood of righteous Abel** unto the blood of Zacharias son of Barachias, whom ye slew between the temple and the altar." (Matthew 23:34-35)

When identifying that "murderer from the beginning," how can we argue when Jesus Christ himself named Abel as the first person murdered upon the earth? Even though some people may argue that the serpent murdered Adam and Eve through her lie, we do not see them counted by Jesus Christ as murders. After all that we have just read, I believe it should be clear that CAIN is that murderer and that liar from the beginning who Jesus was referring to as "the devil."

I will now address the claim that Cain was literally the son of the serpent. People who turn to books such as the Targum, and Gnostic texts like *The Apocryphon of John* (The Secret Book of John), believe the "serpent seed" is a physical seed line due to what those books say. This claim can only be supported using books outside of the Bible because the scripture is clear about who Cain's father is.

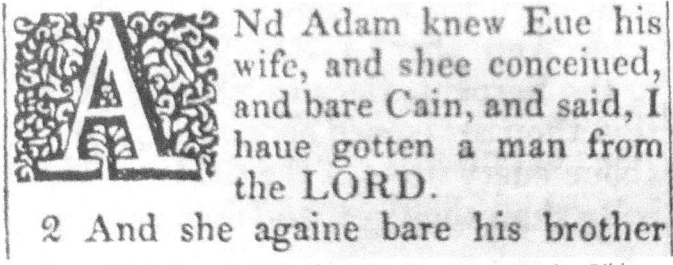

Nd Adam knew Eue his wife, and shee conceiued, and bare Cain, and said, I haue gotten a man from the LORD.

2 And she againe bare his brother

Figure 3-0-1: Genesis 4:1 in the 1611 King James Version Bible.

Genesis 4:1 tells us plainly that Adam is Cain's father. The passage reads: "And Adam knew Eve his wife; and she conceived, and bare Cain, and said, I have gotten a man from the LORD." It's worth noting that the 1611 King James Version Bible did not have a semicolon in this verse. Some teachers of the serpent seed doctrine have made a big deal about the semicolon being in some versions of the Bible but it's also in the verse about Seth's birth, yet no one is claiming the semicolon means anything there. It reads, "And Adam knew his wife again; and she bare a son, and called his name Seth..." (Genesis 4:25) It follows the same structure and flow as Genesis 4:1 which describes the events of Cain's birth. This seems like an open and shut case to me.

Figure 3-0-2: "Adam and Eve" by Giovanni della Robbia (1515) is one of many medieval artworks that depict the serpent in the garden of Eden as female.

CHAPTER 04: THE WISE WOMAN AND THE FOOLISH WOMAN

From here, we will discuss who the SERPENT is. It is her seed that is destined to wage war against the seed of the righteous woman. Yes, there is a seed-war happening in the earth, throughout history, and it is a war between the spiritual children of two women.

If you have never noticed, throughout the Bible there is a theme of a competition between two women. One of these women is righteous, or wise; she represents Eve. Eve's children are the righteous seed of Israel and the gentiles who are grafted in. The Bible tells us that the Dragon made war with the remnant of her seed who kept the commandments of Yahawah (God) and the testimony of Yahawashai (Jesus Christ). We see this woman in Revelation 12.

The other woman being compared is foolish, wicked, and whorish. She is said to be an evil adulteress in the book of Proverbs. I will refer to her as Babylon. This wicked woman has her own children whom God Himself promises to kill. We see her in Revelation chapter 17. Proverbs 14:1 says, "Every **wise woman** buildeth her house: but **the foolish** plucketh it down with her hands." Proverbs 7:4-5 reads, "Say unto **wisdom**, Thou art my sister; and call understanding thy kinswoman: That they may keep thee from **the strange woman**, from the stranger which flattereth with her words."

There is more to say on the "strange woman" whom I shall deal with later in this book. In Matthew 25:1-4, Jesus Christ makes a comparison between wise virgins and foolish virgins. It reads: "Then shall the kingdom of heaven be likened unto ten virgins, which took their lamps, and went forth to meet the bridegroom. And **five of them were wise**, and **five were foolish**. They that were foolish took their lamps, and took no oil with them: But the wise took oil in their vessels with their lamps." (Matthew 25:1-4)

A lamp gives light and represents the commandments of God. We have in this parable given by Jesus Christ an example of two types of people: those who act on their faith and those who are hearers of the word only. Those who acted on their faith, and were obedient to the Father, were ready when the bridegroom came. The foolish had no faith to act on, and did not make it into the wedding. As demonstrated with Rebekah, the two warring seed lines can come from the same womb, proving that it's spiritual:

"And the LORD said unto her, Two nations *are* in thy womb, and **two manner of people** shall be separated from thy bowels..." (Genesis 25:23)

Even though Rebekah was a wise woman herself, her son Esau was spiritually a son of the foolish woman (a seed of the Serpent). Jacob, on the other hand, continued in the faith of his fathers. As God said, according to Romans 9:13, "Jacob have I loved, but Esau have I hated."

In Genesis 3:15, God proclaims to the Serpent, "...I will put enmity between thee and the woman, and between thy seed and her seed; it shall bruise thy head, and thou shalt bruise his heel." Some have claimed that women have no seed but the Bible indicates the opposite in numerous places. The Hebrew word translated as "seed" is ZERA (Strong's H2233). In the context of Genesis 3:15, it means offspring. I'll give you a few examples of ZERA (H2233) being used with women:

"And Adam knew his wife again and she bare a son, and called his name Seth: For God, said <u>she</u>, hath appointed <u>ME</u> another **seed** instead of Abel, whom Cain slew." (Genesis 4:25)

"And they blessed <u>Rebekah</u>, and said unto her, Thou art our sister, be thou the mother of thousands of millions, and let **thy seed** possess the gate of those which hate them." (Genesis 24:60)

"And the angel of the LORD said unto [Hagar], I will multiply **thy seed** exceedingly, that it shall not be numbered for multitude." (Genesis 16:10)

There are more examples of the Bible telling us that women have seed (offspring) but enough has already been shown to prove the point. As part of the war against the Serpent's seed, in numerous places in the Bible, God has promised to kill Babylon's children. In Isaiah 47:8, Babylon says in her heart: "...I am, and none else beside me; I shall not sit as a widow, neither shall I know the loss of **children**." God promises her, in Isaiah 47:9, that the loss of children will come upon her. Jesus Christ says in Revelation 2:23, "...I will kill her **children** with death; and all the churches shall know that I am he which searcheth the reins and hearts."

I understand that people have become comfortable with the idea that this seed-battle is between a male and a female, but the truth has been revealed. And it has been hidden in plain sight for years. For example, in medieval art, the serpent in Eden was often depicted as being female. People's opinions on the possible reasons for this depiction range from the serpent representing Lilith to the serpent being a reflection of Eve, as part of some patriarchal or misogynistic demonization of women. But I believe that depicting the serpent as a female in art was merely a way that the truth could be put out in the open by those who knew the truth, while they upheld the sanctioned doctrine that the serpent was a male, for public consumption. The truth about what happened in the garden of Eden is that the serpent approached Eve—not Adam—because she was another woman; and she wanted to make Eve corrupt like herself.

Figure 4-0-1: Adam, Eve, and the Serpent beneath the Virgin Mary statue at Notre Dame Cathedral.

Figure 4-0-2: Sculptor Pompeo Coppini with Columbia, the *"Goddess of America."*

CHAPTER 05: THE QUEEN OF THE POWER OF THE AIR

"And you hath he quickened, who were dead in trespasses and sins; Wherein in time past ye walked according to the course of this world, according to the prince of the power of the air, the spirit that now worketh in the children of disobedience" (Ephesians 2:1-2)

In this scripture, Paul identifies the spirit of wickedness that is operating in the world contrary to the spirit of God. He calls it the "prince of the power of the air." The Greek word used for "prince" is ARCHON (Strong's G758), which means first in rank, or a ruler. The word used for "power" is exousia (Strong's G1849), which means authority or jurisdiction. The word AER (Strong's G109), used for air, can mean the lower air or the upper atmosphere. So, in other words, we're dealing with a **ruler of the jurisdiction of the upper atmosphere.** Now, where do we see a similar title appear in the Bible? That would be in the book of Jeremiah:

"The children gather wood, and the fathers kindle the fire, and the women knead their dough, to make cakes to the **queen of heaven**, and to pour out drink offerings unto other gods, that they may provoke me to anger." (Jeremiah 7:18)

The prince of the power of the air is the "Queen of Heaven." That is the spirit that now worketh in the children of disobedience. Why else is this significant? It is because the star associated with the Queen of Heaven is **Venus**, and Venus is also called **LUCIFER**. I dare say everyone knows that Venus is the name of a Roman goddess, and that the planet is associated with femininity; the symbol for Venus is even the symbol for female. Venus has long been identified with goddesses, but did you know that those goddesses are named in the Bible?

Ashtoreth is named in the Bible as the goddess of the Zidonians. Her name, when translated, means STAR. Ishtar and Ashtarte are other forms of this same goddess. In Greece, she's called Aphrodite. You won't find any male gods in the Bible that are identified with Venus. So, from now on, we can refer to Venus and understand that it covers all the names and identities of the goddesses who are also known as Lucifer.

While the goddess Asherah is present in the Bible, you won't find her name in most English translations because her name was translated as "grove" and "tree." I won't speculate on why this choice was made by the translators, though I do have some ideas. I will leave that alone and just tell you that Asherah's worship involved planted trees, poles, and groves. She's essentially "mother earth." All of these goddesses mentioned go by the title of the Queen of Heaven. Is there a title more fitting for the rival of the Most High God than the "Queen of Heaven?"

This title reveals the height of Lucifer's rank among spiritual powers. Colossians 1:16 says, "For by him were all things created, that are in heaven, and that are in earth, visible and invisible, whether they be thrones, or dominions, or principalities, or powers..." The highest rank on this list is "thrones," and it's a rank occupied by a king or queen. Lucifer being the "Queen of Heaven" adds context to Jude 1:9 which says, "Yet Michael the archangel, when contending with the devil he disputed about the body of Moses, durst not bring against him a railing accusation, but said, The Lord rebuke thee."

The Egyptian goddess Isis, or Aset, is linked to both Sirius and Venus. Symbols such as the pentagram and the ankh, can be used for both Venus and Sirius. It can even be said that the symbol for female is a variation of the ankh. It's generally believed that the ankh symbol means "life." Life comes from the womb. The symbol for Venus is a symbol for the womb. The symbol for Venus is also known as the goddess's "hand-mirror." According to *New World Encyclopedia*, "Mirrors were often made in the shape of an ankh." Both the ankh and the sign for Venus resemble the sign for the goddess Tanit.

Figure 5-0-1: A symbol for Tanit, the Ankh, and the planet Venus.

Most Bible teachers that I know of say that goddess worship began at the tower of Babel, and that the original Queen of Heaven was a woman named Semiramis, but this isn't true at all; in fact, the opposite is true. The worship of male false gods began at Babel. The worship of the goddess far predates Babylon. Anyone can confirm this to be true with just a little bit of research.

Catalhoyuk is the location where the figure of the corpulent seated woman, who is the predecessor of the later "Great Mother Goddesses," was discovered. While the interdisciplinary group who studied this location and published their observations in *Religion in the Emergence of Civilization: Catalhoyuk as a Case Study* didn't confirm that there was any religion observed there at all, they recognized the importance of Catalhoyuk because of its place in time:

"The aims of the current excavations at Catalhoyuk in central Turkey (7400-6000 BC) are to explore a site of great importance for our understanding of the first steps toward 'civilization' and to understand its art, symbolism, and ritual. The site occurs... **several thousand years before the cities and states of Mesopotamia and Egypt**, to which the term 'civilization' is often applied." (2)

Figure 5-0-2: The Seated Woman of Catalhoyuk is the prototype of the "Great Mother Goddess."

I won't spend a lot of time debunking the Semiramis-Nimrod myth, because something that has zero supporting evidence to be found anywhere shouldn't need to be debunked. A question begs to be asked, however: why would someone who was supposedly so influential get NO mention in the Bible or any pseudepigraphal books?

Alexander Hislop, author of *The Two Babylons*, is the source of the myth that Nimrod had a wife named Semiramis. He also claimed that Semiramis was the "prototype" for the goddesses who were worshiped around the world. He based his hypothesis on writings by Ovid, a poet that wrote interpretations of **mythology**. Hislop's claims were not based on actual history. As Hislop confessed:

"...Ovid himself tells us that it was Semiramis, the first queen of that city, who was believed to have 'surrounded Babylon with a wall of brick.' Semiramis, then, the first deified queen of that city and tower whose top was intended to reach to heaven, must have been the prototype of the goddess who 'first made towers in cities." (30)

There you have it: this myth of Semiramis being Nimrod's wife has no basis in history. Having cleared that up, a woman by the name of Sammu-Ramat, who lived in the 8th century BCE, according to *World History*, is likely the inspiration for Hislop's claim, but she lived many centuries after Nimrod had already died:

"Semiramis is a legendary queen thought to [be] based on the historical Sammu-Ramat (r. 811-806 BCE) the queen regent of the Assyrian Empire who held the throne for her young son Adad Nirari III until he reached maturity. ...there is very little information about what she did and how she went about doing it and some scholars refer to her simply as 'an obscure Assyrian lady of the eighth century B.C. of whom we know nothing for certain except that she is named on an inscription as lady of the palace."

What we can know for certain is that there is an abundance of evidence which suggests that goddess worship predates the establishment of Babylon by at least a thousand years. In stark contrast, **there is no evidence that any male gods existed before Babylon**. In fact, the first pagan male god that we know of is Anu of Babylon. In *Goddess In The Grass: Serpentine Mythology and the Great Goddess*, Linda Foubister says of religion in the pre-historic era:

"In the ancient past, the Great Goddess was worshipped as the personification of the universal life force. <u>Her sacred symbol was the serpent</u>. Over time, as goddess worship was suppressed by the rise of patriarchy, her serpent was devalued, eventually becoming a symbol of evil. Yet the roots of the life-giving, life-taking Serpent Goddess can be seen in prehistoric artifacts and in mythology, folklore, and art...

Unlocking the mysteries of the Serpent Goddess can reveal how myths of the western world trace the dimming power of the Great Goddess over thousands of years, until her replacement by the one male Judeo-Christian god... **Evidence from the Paleolithic Period suggests the theory that prehistoric people worshipped the creative principle in Nature as the Great Goddess**... Hundreds of small female figurines carved from stone, bone, antler, ivory, and fired clay have been found over Europe and Western Asia [known as Venus figures].... In fact, there **are no images that have been found of a Father god throughout the prehistoric record**." (1-2)

In her book, *When God was a Woman*, Merlin Stone confirms that the male gods came along at a later point in time:

"The archaeological artifacts suggest that <u>in all the Neolithic and early Chalcolithic societies</u> the Divine Ancestress, generally referred to by most writers as **the Mother Goddess, was revered as the supreme deity**... Though at first the Goddess appears to have reigned alone, at some yet unknown point in time She acquired a son or brother (depending upon the geographic location), who was also Her lover and consort." (18-19)

I quote Alice Lucy Trent, the author of *The Feminine Universe*, for another witness that the ancient world practiced the female religion:

"Turning from the 'historical' to the 'prehistoric' period—that is to say, to that vast majority of human history for which written records no longer exist or have been rewritten by patriarchal redactors—**the material evidence makes it clear that the religion of the feminine Deity was predominant for thousands of years**." (12)

In *Mysteries of the Ancient World*, by the National Geographic Society, more details are given on which signs of the ancient goddess religion were found:

"Certainly the central deity in Catal religion was a woman. **Female statuettes abound**... In the shrines, along with such male symbols as bull and ram heads and altars decorated with the actual horn cores of bulls, also appear reliefs of a mother goddess. Quite possibly Catal Huyuk's religious life centered on the female fertility and was directed by priestesses." (41)

The lie of goddess worship beginning at Babylon has been told for too long and I must give readers the correct historical record. Given the information provided, the most-likely sequence of events in the history of religion is as follows:

In the pre-flood world, Lucifer was worshiped as the supreme goddess by those who had turned their backs on the one true Creator, Yah. However, the Most High overthrew that world with a great flood, resetting everything with Noah and his sons. With the knowledge that the Most High God was a male—not a female— being established in the post-flood world, Lucifer inspired counterfeit "father gods" to deceive the world, and she then presented herself as either his wife, daughter, or mother. Given the fact that ANU is the oldest known male god and that he was the original supreme deity in Mesopotamia, we must mark this point in time as the beginning of the creation of male false gods. Gods such as Enki, Marduk, Shamash, and Enlil followed after.

Gods in other cultures such as El, Ba'al, Helios, Osiris, and Zeus are all variations of those earlier gods. Many of these gods, such as EL and Ba'al, bore generic titles that simply meant "god" or "lord," strengthening my theory that they were created by Lucifer as counterfeits to the one true God. It's possible that the ancient Israelites who worshiped Ba'al actually believed they were worshiping the true Lord (Yah). Just like many people today believe they're worshiping the true "God," but they do not in reality. The true God has no wife. He has no mother. He has no sister.

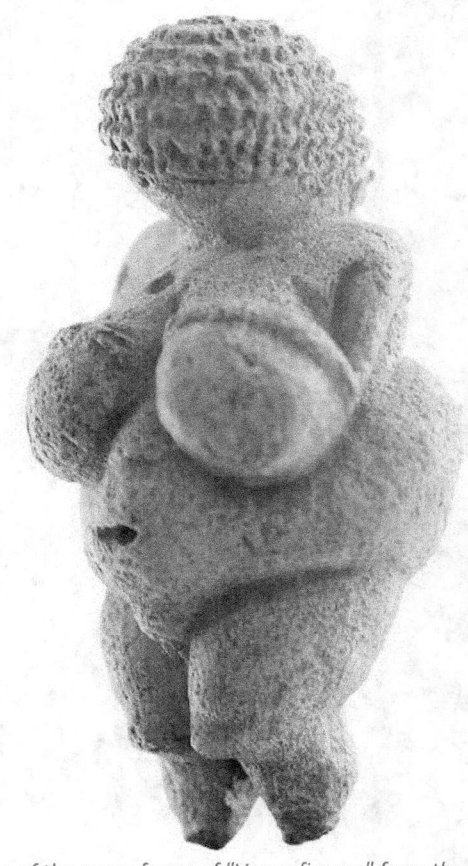

Figure 5-0-3: One of the many forms of "Venus figures" from the pre-historic period.

Figure 5-0-4: Lilith (1887) by John Collier.

CHAPTER 06: THIS IS THEIR EYE

Unbeknownst to many, the true meaning of the "All-Seeing Eye" is revealed in Zechariah chapter five. As I said in an earlier chapter, the angel speaking with the prophet gave the woman called Wickedness another identifier: the **EYE**. In Zechariah 5:6, the angel says, "this is their resemblance through all the earth". This is the only time in the entire Bible that the word A'YAN was translated as "resemblance." The word literally means EYE and the ancient pictograph for a'yan is a drawing of an eye, as shown on *Wikipedia*:

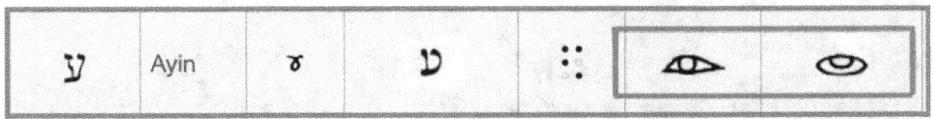

Figure 6-0-1: Highlighted above are the paleo-Hebrew pictographs for A'YAN.

Zechariah 5:6-8 can also be translated as: "... **This is their EYE** through all the earth... this is a woman that sitteth in the midst of the ephah. And he said, This is wickedness." In addition to that, eyes in the Bible can represent spirits; this is demonstrated in the book of Revelation, where it says, "And I beheld, and, lo, in the midst of the throne and of the four beasts, and in the midst of the elders, stood a Lamb as it had been slain, having seven horns and seven eyes, which are the seven Spirits of God sent forth into all the earth." (Revelation 5:6)

The guiding spirit of Freemasonry is called the "Genius of Freemasonry," and it is depicted as a woman. Freemasons often use the symbol of the EYE in their imagery to represent "God." The EYE is also a prominent symbol used by the Illuminati. That makes sense given the fact that the Illuminati uses the goddess's owl as the symbol of their order.

The legendary Christian martyr, Saint Lucy, is known as the "protector of the eyes." On the *St. Lucy Catholic Parish* website, it is explained that: "St. Lucy's legend holds that her eyes were gauged out and God then provided her with new eyes. This came about, it is said, because her pagan suitor loved her beautiful eyes. In some versions of this story, St. Lucy plucked out her eyes herself and gave them to her suitor; in other versions, her eyes were removed by her persecutors. St. Lucy is often depicted holding a small plate with two eyes on it. She is the patron saint of the blind."

Figure 6-0-2: A goddess weeps at a grave in the Old St. Matthew's Churchyard, Berlin, Germany.

What happens with this woman called Wickedness in the book of Zechariah is that she is carried to the land of Shinar (Babylon) and established on her own base (or pedestal). Now, where have we seen the symbol of **an EYE placed on a base**? That would be the pyramid with the unattached capstone. That pyramid with the unattached capstone is on the back of the U.S. dollar.

Figure 6-0-3: The "Eye of Providence" (left) and the Columbia Broadcasting System logo (right).

The spirit of America is called Columbia. She is conflated with the Goddess of Freedom who is perched atop the U.S. Capitol Building. The Columbia Broadcasting System uses the symbol of the EYE as its logo. Everything begins to fall into place once you understand who the goddess is. All these years, the devil was in the details of Zechariah chapter five. In *Masonic and Occult Symbols Illustrated*, Dr. Cathy Burns states:

"Outlining the eye emulates the goddess, who is often portrayed with large, distinctive eyes, capable of seeing through space and time as well as into our innermost hearts. Ishtarte, the Goddess of Light, was known in the ancient Middle East as **the Eye Goddess** because the light she brings from heaven to earth illuminates the world. The Egyptian Goddess Maat originally possessed **the All-Seeing Eye**, which later was transferred to Horus... The Goddess's ability to see and know all things became a terrifying concept in patriarchal times, and her mystical eye was turned into **the 'evil eye,'** associated during the time of the Inquisition with Witches..." (308)

It's ironic that Ma'at was the goddess who held the scales of justice and was identified with the All-Seeing Eye, but she now stands outside of the courtrooms, blindfolded, and it is said that "justice is blind." Barbara G. Walker provides confirming information in *The Woman's Dictionary of Symbols and Sacred Objects*:

"Many figurines of the early Sumerian Eye Goddess (3500-3000 B.C.) have been found in Syria and around the Mediterranean. Like Maat in Egypt, she represented the spirit of truth and law. Hers were the All-Seeing Eyes from which no crime could be hidden. She later merged with the Goddess Mari, who was also depicted with huge staring eyes although her form was more human. Eventually the Eye Goddess developed into the mysterious wise creatress Mari-Ishtar, or Mari-Anna, once worshiped as the consort of Yahweh in Jerusalem. The Goddess's staring eyes aroused uncomfortable feelings in men, who came to look upon her as a spirit of the evil eye." (201)

Figure 6-0-4: Hamsa Hand (Hand of Fatima or Hand of Miriam).

An item that is said to ward off the "evil eye" is a hand-shaped object called the Hamsa Hand. It often features an open eye in its palm. It is also called the Hand of Miriam (Mary), the Hand of Fatima, and the Hand of Venus. It's ironic that an amulet meant to ward off the "evil eye" features the eye of the goddess who is herself "the evil eye." In *The Sign Language of the Mysteries*, J. S. M. Ward says the hand sign of the "horns" (raising only the index finger and the little finger) is widely used "as a protection against the evil eye." (162) This sign is commonly referred to as the "devil horns."

Walker confirms what Ward says about the sign of the horns being used to ward off the evil eye. She says, "To make the devil's horns, as a hand gesture, is one of the oldest prophylactic signs supposed to avert the evil eye and placate harmful powers... Perhaps even more pertinent to the diabolization of the gesture, however, is the fact that **it was once intimately associated with the Goddess**. In India, it is still the sacred mudra (hand gesture) of Jagadamba, which is a title of the Goddess meaning 'Mother of the World.'" (308)

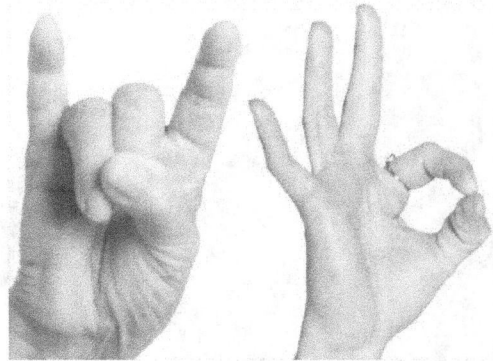

Figure 6-0-4: "The Sign of the Horns" (left) and the "Okay" hand sign (right).

It's unlikely that these signs are used by initiates of the Illuminati or the Freemasons as protection against the evil eye, because they must know that the goddess IS the evil eye. Not only that but touching any of the fingers to the thumb (forming a ring) makes the sign of the Vesica Piscis (womb), even with the "Horns Sign." It's much more likely that these signs are used by initiates to signify that they are protected by her.

Figure 6-0-5: The "Goddess of Mercy" in the distance behind a giant Vesica Piscis (womb) hand sign.

Figure 6-0-6: "Freemasonry instructing the people" (1875). Freemasonry is personified by a goddess.

CHAPTER 07: THE DRAGON RIDES THE BEAST

There are two parties who are blamed for deceiving the entire world: they are Babylon and the Dragon. There are several scriptures that we must observe:

"Babylon hath been a golden cup in the LORD'S hand, **that made all the earth drunken**: the nations have drunken of her wine; therefore the nations are mad." (Jeremiah 51:7)

"And a mighty angel took up a stone like a great millstone, and cast it into the sea, saying, Thus with violence shall that great city Babylon be thrown down, and shall be found no more at all... **for by thy sorceries were all nations deceived**." (Revelation 18:21, 23)

"And the great dragon was cast out, that old serpent, called the Devil, and Satan, **which deceiveth the whole world**..." (Revelation 12:9)

"And I saw an angel come down from heaven, having the key of the bottomless pit and a great chain in his hand. And he laid hold on the dragon, that old serpent, which is the Devil, and Satan, and bound him a thousand years, And cast him into the bottomless pit, and shut him up, and set a seal upon him, that he should **deceive the nations no more**... And when the thousand years are expired, Satan shall be loosed out of his prison, And shall go out to **deceive the nations** which are in the four quarters of the earth" (Revelation 20:1-3, 7-8)

Both Babylon and the Dragon are said to have deceived the nations. It's telling, as I said in the introduction, that only Babylon is arraigned for having deceived the world. She gets three chapters in the book of Revelation dedicated to her judgement. Remember what I said about the Whore of Babylon sharing names with the Queen of Heaven; it reinforces that "MYSTERY Babylon" is not just a city, but the spirit of the goddess who is identified with Babylon (who also just happens to be called Lucifer). To further demonstrate that Babylon is the Dragon, I will show you where Babylon is treated like the Devil herself.

I'll start in Genesis 3:15, where Yahawah said to the Serpent, "...I will put enmity between thee and the woman, and between thy seed and her seed." We see in Revelation 12:17 that the Dragon is trying to destroy the seed of the wise woman (Eve/Israel). In this seed war between two women (Eve the wise woman and Babylon the foolish woman), we see a vision of the Dragon trying to destroy Eve's seed.

Revelation 12:17 says, "And the dragon was wroth with the woman, and went to make war with the remnant of her seed, which keep the commandments of God, and have the testimony of Jesus Christ." Notice that the Bible says that it was **the dragon** who made war with the wise woman's seed; but who is it that is said to be guilty of that bloodshed?

"And a mighty angel took up a stone like a great millstone, and cast it into the sea, saying, Thus with violence shall that great city Babylon be thrown down, and shall be found no more at all... for by thy sorceries were all nations deceived... **And in her was found the blood of prophets, and of saints, and of all that were slain upon the earth**." (Revelation 18:21-24)

In Revelation 18, Babylon is arraigned for deceiving all nations and for her violence against Eve's seed. While it's always man on the earth who is carrying out the violence, they are being driven by spirits to commit those acts. The problem with blaming man here (and the reason this prophecy can't be talking about the natural realm) is that no mortal man has been alive since Abel was slain, neither was there a single bloodline responsible for all the violence against Eve's seed. Only a spirit could have been there from the beginning and took part in all of it; a spirit who was prophesied to have enmity with Eve's seed—that is the Serpent.

Question: why is Babylon guilty of all that blood, and not the Serpent? Is the wrong party being indicted here? Answer: NO! Babylon IS the Serpent. And she has made war with Eve's seed ever since Cain slew Abel! Otherwise, what reason would all the saints who have been killed in ages past have to rejoice when Babylon is thrown down in the end times? As Revelation 18:20 says, "Rejoice over her, thou heaven, and ye holy apostles and prophets; for God hath avenged you on her."

Doesn't it strike you as odd that the saints and those who dwell in Heaven are told to rejoice when God takes vengeance on Babylon but not on the Serpent? Babylon falls and there is rejoicing. The Serpent is thrown into the Lake of Fire and... *cricket noises*. If the Most High Yah has indeed allowed me to understand all of this correctly, then all prophecies against Babylon apply to the Serpent. I will now give you a timeline of events in the book of Revelation concerning the fall of Babylon.

First, we should all fully understand that none of those who are saved and redeemed from the earth by the blood of the Lamb, Jesus Christ (Yahawashai Hamashayach), are appointed to God's wrath. When the Most High pours out His wrath (the bowl judgements), the saved have been taken out of harm's way. So, everything that is happening upon the earth when the bowls begin to be poured out takes place AFTER the last trumpet:

"And the seventh angel sounded; and there were great voices in heaven, saying, The kingdoms of this world are become the kingdoms of our Lord, and of his Christ; and he shall reign for ever and ever." (Revelation 11:15).

This is the **end of the tribulation** of those days; it is followed by the Day of the Lord. The King of Kings and Lord of Lords (Jesus Christ) is returning to claim the kingdoms of the earth. As Revelation 6:17 says, "For the great day of his wrath is come; and who shall be able to stand?" The first bowl that is filled with the wrath of God is poured out in Revelation 16:2:

"And the first went, and poured out his vial upon the earth; and there fell a noisome and grievous sore upon the men which had the mark of the beast, and upon them which worshipped his image." (Revelation 16:2)

In what follows, take note of WHEN "Great Babylon" is judged; it happens AFTER the cities of the nations have already fallen:

"And the seventh angel poured out his vial into the air; and there came a great voice out of the temple of heaven, from the throne, saying, It is done. And there were voices, and thunders, and lightnings; and there was a great earthquake, such as was not since men were upon the earth, so mighty an earthquake, and so great. And the great city was divided into three parts, and the cities of the nations fell: **and great Babylon came in remembrance before God, to give unto her the cup of the wine of the fierceness of his wrath**." (Revelation 16:17-19)

You may have heard people teach that we need to flee Babylon before she is judged, but where are you going to run to? What place on this earth is going to be safe, according to these scriptures? If you have been understanding the timeline correctly, you should know that those who are saved are with Jesus Christ and out of harm's way before the first vial is even poured out. I want to stress that the judgement of Babylon doesn't even happen until AFTER the seventh vial of God's wrath has been poured out. This is a special and unique event that focuses on HER. The Dragon and Serpent get no such special attention. But, of course, as I've already said, that's because **Great Babylon is the Dragon and the Serpent**.

"...and great Babylon came in remembrance before God, to give unto her the cup of the wine of the fierceness of his wrath." (Revelation 16:19)

Like with every prophecy that has two subjects, a natural subject and a supernatural subject, we must rightly divide what's being said and apply it to the correct subject. When Babylon is judged, we know if there truly is a spirit entity who says in her heart, "I sit a queen, and am no widow, and shall see no sorrow," (Revelation 18:7) then to maintain Biblical congruence, that spirit cannot end right there in Revelation 18:21, where it says, "Thus with violence shall that great city Babylon be thrown down, and shall be found no more at all." We know this because she must go into the Lake of Fire. In the natural realm, we can trust that the location of Babylon will indeed be destroyed completely. In the spiritual, we should understand that this is only the end of Babylon's rule.

Immediately after Lucifer is judged in Revelation 18, we see great rejoicing in Revelation 19:

> "And after these things I heard a great voice of much people in heaven, saying, Alleluia; Salvation, and glory, and honour, and power, unto the Lord our God: For true and righteous are his judgments: **for he hath judged the great whore, which did corrupt the earth with her fornication, and hath avenged the blood of his servants at her hand**. And again they said, Alleluia. And her smoke rose up for ever and ever.
>
> And the four and twenty elders and the four beasts fell down and worshipped God that sat on the throne, saying, Amen; Alleluia. And a voice came out of the throne, saying, Praise our God, all ye his servants, and ye that fear him, both small and great. And I heard as it were the voice of a great multitude, and as the voice of many waters, and as the voice of mighty thunderings, saying, Alleluia: for the Lord God omnipotent reigneth." (Revelation 19:1-6)

Babylon is thrown down and the saints rejoice. Later in this chapter, we see the beast and the false prophet are also thrown alive into the Lake of Fire. Then, in Revelation 20, we see the Serpent again:

"And I saw an angel come down from heaven, having the key of the bottomless pit and a great chain in his hand. **And he laid hold on the dragon, that old serpent, which is the Devil, and Satan, and bound him a thousand years**, And cast him into the bottomless pit, and shut him up, and set a seal upon him, that he should deceive the nations no more, till the thousand years should be fulfilled: and after that he must be loosed a little season." (Revelation 20:1-3)

I believe that the fall of the spiritual Babylon is followed immediately by her being bound in the bottomless pit for a thousand years. There will be a rest from her seduction. As Revelation 18:23 says of Babylon, "...for by **thy** sorceries were all nations deceived." And now that she has been sealed in the bottomless pit, she can "deceive the nations no more." (Revelation 20:3)

"And when the thousand years are expired, Satan shall be loosed out of his prison, And shall go out to deceive the nations which are in the four quarters of the earth..." (Revelation 20:7-8)

There won't be any Mother Goddess worship on earth when Lucifer is in the bottomless pit. However, Babylon will be loosed for a short time to resume her sorcery and to deceive the nations again, just before her final fall.

"And **the devil that deceived them** was cast into the lake of fire and brimstone, where the beast and the false prophet are, and shall be tormented day and night for ever and ever." (Revelation 20:10)

I can't help but notice that the words "her smoke rose up for ever and ever," in Revelation 19:3, sounds a lot like what happens when the damned go into the lake of fire. Perhaps this verse skips ahead chronologically, like Revelation 14:11 does: "And the smoke of their torment ascendeth up for ever and ever: and they have no rest day nor night, who worship the beast and his image, and whosoever receiveth the mark of his name." That is the end of the Dragon who rode the beast and deceived all nations, as it is written in the scriptures.

The conceptualization of the goddess Innana as being synonymous with the serpent and dragon can be found in the ancient Mesopotamian writings of Enheduanna, who is cited as the world's earliest known named author. She lived in the city of Ur, where Abraham was from. It is likely that her writings were known to the ancient Israelites. And so, symbols such as the "serpent" and the "dragon" could have been recognized as identifiers of the goddess Inanna (the Queen of Heaven). In some of her collected writings, Enheduanna said of the goddess Inanna:

"Your Queen is Inanna,......, **The Great Dragon** who speaks inimical words to the evil..... who goes against the enemies' land...." (STH 26: 321-323)

In *The Exaltation of Inanna*, composed by Enheduanna, it is written:

"Like a dragon you have deposited venom on the land; when you roar at the earth like Thunder, no vegetation can stand up to you. A flood descending from its mountain, Oh foremost One, you are the Inanna of Heaven and Earth! Raining the fanned fire down upon the nation, endowed with me's by An, **Lady mounted on a Beast**..." (selections from lines 9-65)

What we have here are ancient religious writings from Ur describing Inanna, who is Venus (also called Lucifer), as "the great dragon" and a "lady mounted on a beast". It bears repeating that Mother of Harlots was also a title given to the "Inanna", meaning "Lady of Heaven" (Queen of Heaven). She was the goddess of sacred prostitution, the patron deity of both male and female prostitutes. Keep in mind that male prostitutes adorned in women's attire were referred to as abominations by the Most High God Yah. On top of that, the Queen of heaven was also called the Mother of the Gods. Currently, as the Virgin Mary, she is likewise called the Mother of God. False gods in the Bible are also called abominations. So again, I do not dispute that there is indeed a physical location called Babylon, but as presented, you can see that there is abundant evidence from Biblical Scripture, as well as corroboration from ancient pagan text, that the Great Whore of Babylon is synonymous with the Serpent and the Dragon.

Figure 7-0-1: A Roman coin showing a goddess sitting on seven hills. She is the protectress of Rome.

Figure 7-0-2: The Armada Memorial in Plymouth depicting Britannia.

CHAPTER 08: THE LADY OF KINGDOMS

As the Apostle Paul said in Ephesians 6:12, we wrestle "against principalities, against powers, against the rulers of the darkness of this world, against spiritual wickedness in high places." The Greek word used for "principalities" is ARCHE (Strong's G746). One of the definitions of ARCHE, from *Blue Letter Bible*, is:

"V. the first place, principality, rule, magistracy
    A. of angels and demons"

The meaning behind his statement is that ultimately, our enemies are invisible; they are angels and demonic spirits in the heavens. So as much as people want to argue about the physical location of MYSTERY, Babylon, I am focused on exposing the spirit. There are multiple verses in the Word of God that make clear the fact that the Great Whore of Babylon has conscious thought, aspirations, and a heart. Consider for example the following Scriptures wherein the harlot proclaims:

"I shall be a lady for ever." (Isaiah 47:10)

"I am, and none else beside me; I shall not sit as a widow, neither shall I know the loss of children." (Isaiah 47:8)

"None seeth me... I am, and none else beside me." (Isaiah 47:10)

"I sit a queen, and am no widow, and shall see no sorrow." (Revelation 18:7)

In Zephaniah 2:13,15, a prophecy of destruction is spoken against the city of Nineveh. In this text, we find that corresponding words are spoken by the "virgin daughter of Babylon". It reads:

"And he will stretch out his hand against the north, and destroy Assyria; and will make Nineveh a desolation, and dry like a wilderness... This is the rejoicing city that dwelt carelessly, that **said in her heart, I am, and there is none beside me**..."

This is another profound example of a prophecy with a spiritual fulfillment. The principality over Nineveh speaks boldly, declaring that there is none beside her. Joshua J. Mark, from *World History*, says that the city of Nineveh "...had become an important religious centre for worship of the goddess Ishtar. The meaning of the name is disputed but most likely relates to the prefix Nin or Nina which often appears in the names of deities... and could have meant 'House of the Goddess' or, specifically, 'House of Ishtar' as **the city was associated with that goddess from an early date**."

It comes to me as no surprise to find that a city which said in her heart, "I am, and there is none else beside me" was a stronghold for the goddess, even as documented in this secular historic text. This is merely one of many examples of how diligent objective historical research serves to validate my own uncommon understanding of the central importance of the prominent feminine entity that is known Biblically as Mystery Babylon.

In Revelation 17:18, an angel spoke with John and proclaimed, "And the woman which thou sawest is that great city, which reigneth over the kings of the earth." That's a curious thing to say, is it not? Do not kings usually reign over cities? How can a city reign over all the kings of the earth? Who reigns over that city then? It should be obvious in this verbiage that we are dealing with a PRINCIPALITY here; a principality that goes all the way back to the beginning and shares the name of the city BABYLON. According to *Ancient Origins*:

"The Ishtar Gate is so named, because it was dedicated to the Babylonian goddess Ishtar... **Her cult was the most important one in ancient Babylon**; it is believed to have included temple prostitution, although this is debatable. According to the noted Assyriologist Samuel Noah Kramer, kings in the ancient Near Eastern region of Sumer established their legitimacy by taking part in <u>a ritual sexual act in the temple of the fertility goddess Ishtar</u> every year on the tenth day of the New Year festival Akitu."

Not only is the goddess synonymous with Babylon but, as I just shared, kings established their legitimacy to the throne by committing fornication with the sacred prostitutes in the Queen of Heaven's temple. Does this not provide a very clear and literal example of what the Bible refers to as the kings of the earth committing fornication with her.

"And there came one of the seven angels which had the seven vials, and talked with me, saying unto me, Come hither; I will shew unto thee the judgment of the great whore that sitteth upon many waters: **With whom the kings of the earth have committed fornication**, and the inhabitants of the earth have been made drunk with the wine of her fornication." (Revelation 17:1-2)

What we are dealing with here are literal acts of fornication involving kings and priestesses (the embodiment of the goddess on earth) in worship of the Queen of Heaven; that is what Revelation chapter 17:2 is referring to. The Bible says two more times that this ritual act of fornication took place:

"...For all nations have drunk of the wine of the wrath of her fornication, and **the kings of the earth have committed fornication with her**..." (Revelation 18:3)

"And **the kings of the earth, who have committed fornication** and lived deliciously with her, shall bewail her..." (Revelation 18:9)

There is even more proof that the Queen of Heaven is in fact the Dragon who puts kings on the throne! Isis, **whose name means THRONE**, is regarded as the throne that all kings reign upon. She is often depicted with a throne on her head. Every king is pictured as the child Horus sitting on her lap. If you were not her son, you were not a king.

Figure 8-0-1: Horus sitting on his first throne, the lap of Isis.

Revelation 13:2 says of the Beast that comes out of the sea, "...the dragon gave him his power, and his seat, and great authority." The Greek word for "seat" is THRONOS (G2362) and it means THRONE. The woman riding the beast sits on seven mountains—not hills, mountains! Why is this important? It's because mountains in the Bible are prophetically symbolic of KINGDOMS. Revelation 17:9-10 says, "The seven heads are seven **mountains**, on which the woman sitteth. And there are seven **kings.**"

Jesus Christ spoke of a spiritual mountain, or kingdom, in Matthew 11:23, when he said, "For verily I say unto you, That whosoever shall say unto this **mountain**, Be thou removed, and be thou cast into the sea; and shall not doubt in his heart, but shall believe that those things which he saith shall come to pass; he shall have whatsoever he saith." He demonstrated that when he sent the unclean spirits out of a man and into some swine, who then ran into the sea and were drowned.

Because there are seven kingdoms that the woman sits on, there are seven kings mentioned in Revelation 17:10. Additional verses that demonstrate the fact that mountains represent kingdoms can be found in the book of Daniel:

"...and the stone that smote the image became a great **mountain**, and filled the whole earth... And in the days of these kings shall the God of heaven set up a **kingdom**, which shall never be destroyed: and the kingdom shall not be left to other people, but it shall break in pieces and consume all these kingdoms, and it shall stand for ever." (Daniel 2:35, 44)

The Virgin Mary is called the Lady of All Nations. Nations is just another word for Kingdoms. Isaiah 47:5 says, "Sit thou silent, and get thee into darkness, O daughter of the Chaldeans: for thou shalt no more be called, The lady of kingdoms." Consider the symbolism of the Ishtar Gate; it represented Ishtar's protection of the city and the people within it. The Queen of Heaven is the protectress of kingdoms, sitting on the mountains of the present and the past. Let's compare this with Luke 4:5-6 when the Devil tried to tempt Jesus Christ. It reads:

"And the devil, taking him up into an high mountain, shewed unto him all the kingdoms of the world in a moment of time. And the devil said unto him, All this power will I give thee, and the glory of them: for that is delivered unto me; and to whomsoever I will I give it." (Luke 4:5-6)

Was the fact that the Devil took Jesus up to a high **mountain** to tempt him just another clue as to WHO the Devil was? The goddess Kybele is called the Mountain Mother (Matar Kubileya), after all. As a predecessor of hers, Ninhursag's name meant "lady of the sacred mountain." She was also called

46

"Mamma" and "Mami." Like Kybele, she was also depicted seated on a throne. In *The Great Cosmic Mother: Rediscovering the Religion of the Earth*, the authors make the connection between the mountain goddess and the throne that kings reign from:

> "All the great mountains were seen as the Goddess 'sitting' on the earth. The mountain was the original throne-womb; it combines the symbols of earth, cave, bulk, height, and immortality. In the towering mountain overlooking the land is embodied the enormous strength of the Goddess. Throughout Thracian, Macedonian, Greek and Cretan lands are mountains with huge thrones at their summits, carved laboriously from the rock. **These are the 'empty thrones' waiting for the Goddess to take her seat**. ...Egyptian paintings and statues depict the small, mortal king sitting on the throne-lap of the huge Goddess Isis. In this way the king was reborn, or made immortal, and thereby given the sacred power to rule over the people. He had true power only as her son." (72)

The city of Constantinople, which was the capital of the eastern leg of the Roman empire and is where the legendary Hagia Sophia was built, was devoted to the "Mother of God." Because of the Virgin's protection, the city seemed to have an "immunity," as John Harris puts it in his book *Constantinople: Capital of Byzantium*. He also reveals how strong the confidence in Mary was:

> "The deeds of Constantine and Justinian were not the only ingredients in the potent myth of the Queen of Cities... Constantinople enjoyed special divine protection and the 'God-guarded city' became yet another of its many epithets. When it came to guarding though, it would appear that God delegated the task to the figure whose cult in Byzantium was second only to that of Christ himself, the Virgin Mary. As one contemporary put it: 'About our city you shall know: until the end she will fear no nation whatsoever, for no one will entrap or capture her, not by any means, **for she has been given to the Mother of God** and no one will snatch her out of Her hands. Many nations will break their horns against her walls and withdraw with shame." (39-40)

One of the reasons that we don't identify this goddess who reigns over the kings of the earth in many dual prophecies (prophecies aimed at both a natural and a supernatural subject) is that many of them are addressed primarily to male subjects. We tend to interpret the prophecies as if the spiritual subject is the only subject. We see this in relation to common interpretations of Isaiah chapter 14. As I have said already, the name "Lucifer" is a reference to the star Venus. But only part of this prophecy applies to the subject in the heavens, while the rest of it applies to King Nebuchadnezzar on the earth. Let's talk about where we should draw the lines. In Isaiah 14, we read:

"How art thou fallen from heaven, O **Lucifer**, son of the morning! how art thou cut down to the ground, which didst weaken the nations! For thou hast said in thine heart, I will ascend into heaven, I will exalt my throne above the stars of God: I will sit also upon the mount of the congregation, in the sides of the north: I will ascend above the heights of the clouds; I will be like the most High." (Isaiah 14:12-14)

The "mount of the congregation" could be a reference to earthly Jerusalem, but the words "in the sides of the north" and "above the heights of the clouds" lead us to the conclusion that this is the heavenly Jerusalem being talked about. It's God's kingdom in Heaven. The star Venus rises toward the north in the morning until it is outshined by the sun (a symbol—when understood righteously—for Jesus Christ, who is the light of the world; See John 8:12, Revelation 1:16, 2 Samuel 23:4, Isaiah 60:19). Venus only ascends so far toward the north and then, as the evening star, it falls (just like Babylon).

"Yet thou shalt be brought down to hell, to the sides of the pit." (Isaiah 14:15)

We know that the Devil will be sealed in the bottomless pit for 1,000 years (Revelation 20:3), so Isaiah 14:15 could possibly apply to the spiritual subject as well. However, I believe the verses that follow apply—primarily or entirely—to the historic king Nebuchadnezzar.

"They that see thee shall narrowly look upon thee, and consider thee, saying, Is this the man that made the earth to tremble, that did shake kingdoms; That made the world as a wilderness, and destroyed the cities thereof; that opened not the house of his prisoners?" (Isaiah 14:16-17)

Those that see this king are astonished that one so mighty got brought down so low. For the most part, they seem unimpressed by him. In contrast, I don't believe anyone who sees the spiritual Lucifer will be unimpressed by what they see; we're talking about a being who led astray a third of the angels in heaven.

Verse 18 and 19 confirm that the king who has been brought down into the pit in verse 16 is Nebuchadnezzar who has no glory when he dies.

"All the kings of the nations, even all of them, lie in glory, every one in his own house. But thou art cast out of thy grave like an abominable branch, and as the raiment of those that are slain, thrust through with a sword, that go down to the stones of the pit; as a carcase trodden under feet." (Isaiah 14:18-19)

In conclusion, as far as Isaiah chapter 14 is concerned: only verses 12 through 15 can be fulfilled by Babylon. If we look at what has been accomplished by the goddess already, especially in the form of the Virgin Mary, **she has already fulfilled verses 13 and 14**. Again, the reference to the star Venus (Lucifer) is what makes this prophecy stand out as having two subjects.

Turning to another well-known prophecy, Ezekiel 28, a lamentation is given for Ithobaal III (the Prince and King of Tyre). There are not clear lines between the natural and the spiritual subjects here. In what follows I will provide a careful analysis of verses 1 through 19 with particular focus on who is being addressed. After consideration of these verses, I will discuss how much of the passage appears to be in clear reference to Lucifer, and to the spirit of Babylon. Verses 1 through 9 describe an earthly ruler, referred to as the prince of Tyrus. He is described as prideful and he sets his heart as the heart of God. He is said to have beauty and brightness, in regard to his great wisdom, and his heart was lifted up because of it:

"Son of man, say unto the prince of Tyrus, Thus saith the Lord GOD; Because thine heart is lifted up, and thou hast said, I am a God, I sit in the seat of God, in the midst of the seas; yet thou art a man, and not God, though thou set thine heart as the heart of God: Behold, thou art wiser than Daniel; there is no secret that they can hide from thee: With thy wisdom and with thine understanding thou hast gotten thee riches, and hast gotten gold and silver into thy treasures: By thy great wisdom and by thy traffick hast thou increased thy riches, and thine heart is lifted up because of thy riches:

Therefore thus saith the Lord GOD; Because thou hast set thine heart as the heart of God; Behold, therefore I will bring strangers upon thee, the terrible of the nations: and they shall draw their swords against the beauty of thy wisdom, and they shall defile thy brightness. They shall bring thee down to the pit, and thou shalt die the deaths of them that are slain in the midst of the seas. Wilt thou yet say before him that slayeth thee, I am God? but thou shalt be a man, and no God, in the hand of him that slayeth thee." (Ezekiel 28:1-9)

As it says in verse 9, King Ithobaal's heart was lifted up because of the riches that he got by his "traffick." In verse 11, however, the subject addressed is shifted from the "prince of Tyre" to the "King of Tyre", and in verses 12 and 13 that follow, words are used that clearly indicate the shift to a spiritual subject.

"Son of man, take up a lamentation upon the king of Tyrus, and say unto him, Thus saith the Lord GOD; Thou sealest up the sum, full of wisdom, and perfect in beauty. **Thou hast been in Eden the garden of God**; every precious stone was thy covering, the sardius, topaz, and the diamond, the beryl, the onyx, and the jasper, the sapphire, the emerald, and the carbuncle, and gold: the workmanship of thy tabrets and of thy pipes was prepared in thee in the day that thou wast created." (Ezekiel 28:12-13)

This verse can still apply to historic king Ithobaal III who was full of wisdom and beautiful (Ezekiel 28:7). One thing we don't know is if Ithobaal has ever been in Eden. The location of Eden may be a mystery to us in modern times but I believe that it was known in ancient times. It does seem that this verse might be directed towards a spirit, but one thing that stands out is that there are no sins listed in relation to being in Eden. If this was the Serpent in the garden, you would think that deceiving Eve would be worth a mention here. For the record, in Genesis 3:24, God placed two cherubims at the east of the garden to protect the way to the Tree of Life. At the very least, we know that there were two other cherubims in the garden of Eden.

There are 9 stones listed in these verses. It's unlikely to be a high priest's breastplate, which has 12 stones, and it's much more likely that these stones are being worn purely for their beauty. In corresponding fashion, we see in Revelation 17:4 that Babylon is adorned with precious stones. It reads, "And the woman was arrayed in purple and scarlet colour, and decked with gold and precious stones and pearls, having a golden cup in her hand..." That is something to keep in mind as we continue reading:

"**Thou art the anointed cherub that covereth**; and I have set thee so: thou wast upon the holy mountain of God; thou hast walked up and down in the midst of the stones of fire. Thou wast perfect in thy ways from the day that thou wast created, till iniquity was found in thee." (Ezekiel 28:14-15)

I know of no instances in the Bible when a human was called a cherub. Accordingly, this is the first verse in Ezekiel 28 that I can say with certainty is addressing a spiritual subject. I will come back to this passage later, but let us first consider a few additional verses:

"By the multitude of thy merchandise they have filled the midst of thee with violence, and thou hast sinned: therefore I will cast thee as profane out of the mountain of God: and I will destroy thee, O covering cherub, from the midst of the stones of fire." (Ezekiel 28:16)

It can be seen that it is because of the subject's riches (the multitude of their merchandise), that they have sinned. Verses 13 through 16 could apply to either (or both) Ithobaal III and the "covering cherub." How does this relate to Babylon? Revelation 16:3 says of the Great Whore, "...the merchants of the earth are waxed rich through the abundance of her delicacies." This thus serves as yet another point of profound congruence between Babylon and the "covering cherub" of Ezekiel 28.

Ezekiel proclaimed that King Ithobaal's heart was lifted up because of his beauty, and on the spiritual level, the covering cherub was likewise described as beautiful. What is very curious about that is the fact that no other description of a cherub in the Bible makes them out to be beautiful. As it is written in Ezekiel 10:

"And [the cherubims's] whole body, and their backs, and their hands, and their wings, and the wheels, were full of eyes round about, even the wheels that they four had... And every one had four faces: the first face was the face of a cherub, and the second face was the face of a man, and the third the face of a lion, and the fourth the face of an eagle." (Ezekiel 10:12-14)

After reading that description, it seems odd to me that God would describe a cherub as "beautiful". It makes me wonder if there are other types of cherubims that look different from that which is described in Ezekiel chapter 10, because, honestly, these sound quite frightening to look upon. Ezekiel 28:12 gives a much different description, saying, "Thou sealest up the sum, full of wisdom, and **perfect in beauty**."

And Ezekiel 28:17 adds, "**Thine heart was lifted up because of thy beauty**, thou hast corrupted thy wisdom by reason of thy brightness..." What conclusion can we draw other than that God created different types of cherubs; cherubs who may be so beautiful that they would inspire awe in people who see them. In Revelation 17:6, when John saw Babylon, he wrote, "... and when I saw her, **I wondered with great admiration**." John marveled at the woman with "admiration." She must have been a beautiful sight to behold to captivate him so much. Proverbs 6:25 warns us of the "strange woman," who profoundly appears to be a type and shadow, if not a direct reference to Babylon, and it reads: "**Lust not after her beauty** in thine heart; neither let her take thee with her eyelids."

Could Babylon the Great be a cherub too? Note how the goddess Isis is often portrayed in Egypt in a role as like a "covering cherub." Indeed, she covers the king on the throne, spreading her wings over him like the cherubs spread their wings over the ark of the covenant. Furthermore, she is also known as a goddess of wisdom. According to *Blue Letter Bible*, in the phrase, "<u>anointed</u> cherub that covereth," the Hebrew word translated as anointed is MIMSAH (Strong's H4473). It is defined as, "in the sense of expansion; outspread (i.e. **with outstretched wings**):—anointed." It gives the idea that this cherub stretches out its wings and covers. Does that not invoke the image of Isis?

Figure 8-0-2: Isis is recognizable as the goddess with spread wings.

Figure 8-0-3: Isis covering Osiris with her wings at Isis Temple (photo by Kim Bach).

Moving on to the rest of the chapter, verses 18-19 appear to apply only to king Ithobaal III, if only for the nature of the punishment:

"Thou hast defiled thy sanctuaries by the multitude of thine iniquities, by the iniquity of thy traffick; therefore will I bring forth a fire from the midst of thee, it shall devour thee, and I will bring thee to ashes upon the earth in the sight of all them that behold thee. All they that know thee among the people shall be astonished at thee: thou shalt be a terror, and never shalt thou be any more." (Ezekiel 28:17-19)

It is entirely possible that "being brought to ashes" can be directed to King Ithobal III as well as Babylon. Babylon is prophesied to be burned with fire (Isaiah 47:14 and Revelation 18:8), and we know that her spirit will go into the lake of fire. However, being brought to ashes implies that the subject's body is mortal. In conclusion, like with Isaiah 14, if this prophecy in Ezekiel 28 has a second subject (a spiritual one), it is only addressed in a few verses. The verses that I feel most confident in saying apply to the Great Whore of Babylon are:

"...Thus saith the Lord GOD; Thou sealest up the sum, **full of wisdom, and perfect in beauty**. Thou hast been in Eden the garden of God; **every precious stone was thy covering**... Thou art the **anointed cherub that covereth**; and I have set thee so: thou wast upon the holy mountain of God; thou hast walked up and down in the midst of the stones of fire. Thou wast perfect in thy ways from the day that thou wast created, till iniquity was found in thee. By **the multitude of thy merchandise** they have filled the midst of thee with violence, and thou hast sinned: therefore I will cast thee as profane out of the mountain of God: and I will destroy thee, O covering cherub, from the midst of the stones of fire. **Thine heart was lifted up because of thy beauty**, thou hast corrupted thy wisdom by reason of thy brightness..." (Ezekiel 28:12-17)

54

CHAPTER 09: THE GOD OF FORCES

In Acts chapter 19, verses 26 and 27, Paul confronts the worshipers of Diana in Ephesus. In this text, we see that Diana is referred to as "the great goddess." It is important to note that this very same term can be found in reference to the goddess Kybele, a much earlier moniker given in reference to the enthroned mother goddess in the ancient (pre-historic) period. Indeed, Kybele is also called the "Magna Mater" which means "great mother". On her head is the turreted crown which represents the walls of a city. Notice once again that the goddess is connected to CITIES.

In Daniel 11:38, there is a mention of a "God of Forces" that a western king will glorify. It reads, "But in his estate shall he honour the **God of forces**: and a god whom his fathers knew not shall he honour with gold, and silver, and with precious stones, and pleasant things." That word "forces" is, in Hebrew, MA'OWZ (Strong's H4581). It is defined as: "place or means of safety, protection, refuge, stronghold". Other definitions include a fortified place, a fort or fortress, or even a ROCK.

Figure 9-0-1: The goddesses Kybele and Diana (center) wearing the turreted crowns.

Kybele and other goddesses have been symbols of cities and kingdoms throughout history. The turreted crown on their heads proudly broadcast their role as the protector of that city and everyone in it. As Demetrius the silversmith said in Acts 19:27, "all Asia and the world" worships "the great goddess Diana".

This area called Asia, currently called Turkey, is also where large rocks that have fallen from the sky were worshiped in association with the "great goddess". We see such a rock mentioned in Acts chapter 19.

"And when the townclerk had appeased the people, he said, Ye men of Ephesus, what man is there that knoweth not how that the city of the Ephesians is a worshipper of the great goddess Diana, and of **the image which fell down from [heaven]**?" (Acts 19:35)

The worship of the Queen of Heaven is continued in Mecca at the Kaaba, and it can be proven through an abundance of evidence that Islam is a goddess religion. In *Arabian Religion Before Muhammad*, Dr. Brian Bradford states:

"These accounts of the black stone idol are further corroborated by those given by John of Damascus in the early 8th century in his *Fount of Knowledge, On Heresies*. John reveals that, in his time, he understood the black stone within the Kaaba in Mecca to be nothing more than **the head of an Aphrodite [Al-Uzza] idol** which the Arabs used to worship and called it Kabir, meaning 'great' in Arabic. John also mentioned that 'even to present day, traces of the carving are visible on it to careful observers." (3-4)

The authors of *The Great Cosmic Mother: Rediscovering the Religion of the Earth* reveal that a trinity of goddesses were worshiped in pre-islamic Arabia. Indeed, one of these goddesses, named "Al-Uzza", was the embodiment of Venus, also called Aphrodite in Greece:

"The Threefold Goddess of Arabia [Al-Uzza, Al-Lat and Manat], Magna Dea, was enshrined in the sacred Black Stone, the Kaaba at Mecca, where she was served in ancient times by her priestesses. The sacred Black Stone at Mecca, site of so many pilgrimages, is imprinted with her vulva/yoni sign, and covered with a black pall called 'the skirt of Kaaba.' The male priests who serve her today are called Beni Shaybah, which means '**the sons of the Old Woman**,' i.e., the moon." (156)

Since we will be discussing the "**yoni**" signs and symbolism often, let us be clear about what it is. The yoni, according to *Britannica*, means "abode,' 'source,' '**womb**,' or '**vagina**' in Hinduism." It is "**the symbol of the goddess Shakti**, the feminine generative power." The connection to the abode or the dwelling place is significant, and it occurs often, such as with the Kaaba and it being a dwelling place for gods. The "black rock" represented a type of dwelling place for the goddess in Pergamum. In *The Cult of the Black Virgin*, Ean Begg gives us more information on the meteorites worshiped in association with goddesses:

"Cybele is the Phrygian mother of the gods whose prototype has been traced back to the neolithic matriarchal civilization of Catal Huyuk. She was first worshipped as a black stone, and in was thus that she journeyed to Rome in 205 BC, sent by King Attalus of Pergamum at the request of the Senate... In Pessinus, **the black stone, which in Rome became the head of the goddess, was considered to be her throne**... Her name is etymologically linked with the words for crypt, cave, head and dome and is distantly related to the Ka'aba, the cube-shaped holy of holies in Mecca that contains the feminine black stone venerated by Islam." (56-57)

Whether this black rock in the Kaaba is the same that traveled from Pergamum to Rome is unclear to me, but what is so interesting about these stones is that they were worshiped as the **throne** of the goddess. In Revelation 2:13, Jesus Christ proclaims that Pergamum is where Satan's seat was. The text reads, "I know thy works, and where thou dwellest, even where **Satan's seat** is: and thou holdest fast my name, and hast not denied my faith, even in those days wherein Antipas was my faithful martyr, who was slain among you, where Satan dwelleth." (Revelation 2:13)

That black rock marked the places where the goddess dwelled. Another indicator that goddess worship was a major factor in Pergamum is that Jesus Christ proclaims to the church there: "But I have a few things against thee, because thou hast there them that hold the doctrine of Balaam, who taught Balac to cast a stumblingblock before the children of Israel, to eat things sacrificed unto idols, and to commit fornication." (Revelation 2:14)

As seen here, the doctrine of Balaam involved committing fornication and idolatry. We know Biblically that the worship of Ba'al and Asherah go hand-in-hand (see Judges 3:7 and 6:25). In his admonition against the church of Pergamum, Jesus Christ thus equates goddess worship with Satan worship. And his description of the pagan practices of Balaam directly corroborates with those of the old, perverted goddess religion involving fornication with the priestesses of the Queen of Heaven. This no doubt also corresponds to that which was going on in the church of Thyatira as well. As Revelation 2:20-22 reads:

"Notwithstanding I have a few things against thee, because thou sufferest that woman Jezebel, which calleth herself a prophetess, to teach and to seduce my servants to commit fornication, and to eat things sacrificed unto idols. And I gave her space to repent of her fornication; and she repented not. Behold, I will cast her into a bed, and them that commit adultery with her into great tribulation, except they repent of their deeds." (Revelation 2:20-22)

Here yet again we see that the act of committing fornication is connected with idolatry. We see here that the woman responsible for teaching this form of religion called herself "a prophetess". This tells me that she was a **sacred prostitute** of the goddess. It is unlikely that she was actually named Jezebel; it's more likely that Jesus Christ called her that because the same spirit that was working in Jezebel was working in her. Therefore, this is ultimately an admonition against the doctrine of Lucifer. After all, Jesus Christ called this doctrine the "depths of Satan".

"And I will kill her children with death; and all the churches shall know that I am he which searcheth the reins and hearts: and I will give unto every one of you according to your works. But unto you I say, and unto the rest in Thyatira, as many as have not this doctrine, and which have not known **the depths of Satan**, as they speak; I will put upon you none other burden." (Revelation 2:23-24)

If this earthly woman that Jesus called "Jezebel" had literal children, she may well have sacrificed them to an idol as part of her religious doctrine. As such the threat to "kill her children" would be of little consequence. It seems that this threat to "kill her children" was not aimed at an earthly Jezebel, but at the spiritual Jezebel—**Lucifer**!

Figure 9-0-2: The protector of Sweden, Mother Svea. One of many forms of the goddess who rules over all kingdoms.

Figure 9-0-3: "Venus with Apple" by Bertel Thorvaldsen (1805). The apple symbolizes the "forbidden fruit" and is an object associated with Venus, the Goddess of Love.

CHAPTER 10: THE SPIRIT OF WHOREDOMS

If you were to say out loud, "MYSTERY Babylon is a SPIRIT," there are bound to be those who will disagree with you. But have those critics not heard of the "spirit of whoredoms"? If so then surely they have chosen to arbitrarily disregard and dismiss it with little thought. As I see it, if there is a spirit of whoredoms that leads people away from the one true God Yahawah (as clearly indicated in the Word of God), then why couldn't "the Great Whore" be a spirit too? Why couldn't she be that same SPIRIT of WHOREDOMS? In the book of Hosea, we are presented with two witnesses that a spirit of whoredoms does in fact exist, and so too do we clearly see its connection to goddess worship:

"My people <u>ask counsel at their stocks</u>, and their staff declareth unto them: for the **spirit of whoredoms** hath caused them to err, and they have gone a whoring from under their God. They sacrifice upon the tops of the mountains, and burn incense upon the <u>hills, under oaks and poplars and elms</u>, because the shadow thereof is good: therefore your daughters shall <u>commit whoredom</u>, and <u>your spouses shall commit adultery</u>." (Hosea 4:12-19)

"They will not frame their doings to turn unto their God: for the **spirit of whoredoms** is in the midst of them, and they have not known the LORD." (Hosea 5:4)

The sins committed under the influence of the spirit of whoredoms involved the seeking of counsel from stocks, which were either **sacred trees** or sacred objects of wood. They also sacrificed at the tops of mountains and burned incense under trees, and **they engaged in fornication**. In what follows, we will see in Isaiah 57 that the Israelites committed fornication and enflamed themselves with idols under green trees. The spirit that influenced them is referred to by a different title in this passage, and we will see that there is a reference to a goddess:

"But draw near hither, ye sons of **the sorceress**, the seed of the adulterer and the whore. Against whom do ye sport yourselves? against whom <u>make ye a wide mouth, and draw out the tongue</u>? are ye not children of transgression, a seed of falsehood, Enflaming yourselves with idols under every green tree, slaying the children in the valleys under the clifts of the rocks? ...Upon a lofty and high

mountain hast thou set thy bed: even thither wentest thou up to offer sacrifice."
(Isaiah 57:3-5,7)

Here we have a direct and obvious reference to the goddess **Kali** who sticks her tongue out. This is a universally recognized gesture from her, and the Most High God calls her **THE SORCERESS**. It's very important that we grasp that which is before us. Here we are presented with the "sorceress" Kali, who we know to be another name and face for the Queen of Heaven, and we have her "sons" (or children) mentioned. With that in mind, consider how in Isaiah 47:9, God promises to kill Babylon's children for the multitude of her "sorceries." And in Revelation 18:23, an angel speaks against Babylon, saying, "for by thy sorceries were all nations deceived." There is no doubt in my mind that this "SORCERESS" in Isaiah 57 is the spirit of Babylon.

As Isaiah 57:4 said, the gesture of making a wide mouth and sticking out the tongue (emblematic for Kali) is meant to be a boast against YAH who is God Almighty. We see that the worshipers under the influence of this goddess set their beds on a high mountain to commit fornication and offer sacrifice. This fornication leads to child sacrifice. God calls the fornicators involved "children of transgression," or children of **wickedness**.

Figure 10-0-1: The goddess Kali was projected onto the Empire State Building in New York in 2015.

The Sign Language of the Mysteries author, J. S. M. Ward, adds some interesting observations to consider. He says, "...vulgar little girls put out their tongues. It is quite true that the fair sex have not the monopoly of this insulting gesture, for little boys also adopt it, but speaking generally, **it is more often used by girls**..." (104)

Figure 10-0-2: A screenshot from the music video for "California" by Delta Spirit (Rounder Records).

In the music video for the song "*California*" by Delta Spirit, a young girl with a nose piercing with chain attached (as like the goddess Kali), sticks out her tongue over a flame. The flame comes from the lighter in her hand, which is a type of torch. Accordingly, she is a "light-bearer"—the literal meaning of "Lucifer". California is a combination of two words: the name of the goddess, Kali, and fornia. I believe fornia comes from porneia, which is Greek for "fornication." Esoterically, California could thus quite literally be translated "Kali fornication." Does it really come as a surprise then that the Red Hot Chili Peppers have released a song with that very title?

My hypothesis for why females, especially the rebellious types, are more prone to make a wide mouth and draw out the tongue is that it is a gesture of lewdness. The mouth is an orifice and, for women, opening the mouth for others to see can be sexually suggestive or immodest. This is a way that the same nature of the spirit of whoredoms manifests in women. In the book of Proverbs, we see extensive and recurrent reference to a woman who is called the "strange woman." This woman is the spirit of Babylon. As usual, profound insights can be found with a deeper analysis of the original text. The Hebrew word translated as "strange" is NAKRI (Strong's H5237); it can mean ALIEN, foreign, different (as of kind), and even refer to a HARLOT. We are warned to keep the commandments of Yah because they will protect us from this woman who is on the hunt for a prey like a roaring lion.

Figure 10-0-3: A screenshot from "Electric Love" by Børns (2014), showing symbols of the Spirit of Whoredoms.

"For the commandment is a lamp; and the law is light; and reproofs of instruction are the way of life: To keep thee from **the evil woman**, from the flattery of the tongue of **a strange woman**. Lust not after her beauty in thine heart; neither let her take thee with her eyelids. For by means of a whorish woman a man is brought to a piece of bread: and **the adulteress** will hunt for the precious life." (Proverbs 6:23-26)

There's something very fascinating about the following descriptions that are given in reference to the strange woman of Proverbs. The Word of God speaks of her in ways reminiscent of the goddess, even drawing connections to the abyss and the grave; both being prominent metaphors for the womb in the pagan mysteries.

"For a whore is a **deep ditch**; and a strange woman is a narrow **pit**. She also lieth in wait as for a prey, and increaseth the transgressors among men." (Proverbs 23:27-28)

"**The mouth of strange women is a deep pit**: he that is abhorred of the LORD shall fall therein." (Proverbs 22:14)

The "deep" or the "abyss" were personified by goddesses going back at least as far as Mesopotamia, before being supplanted in the role by male gods such as Enki. In *Ancient Mirrors of Womanhood*, Merlin Stone explains that the image of the sea serpent which dwells in the deep has been linked with numerous goddesses in the past. She says, "The portrayal of Bachue as a woman—and as a serpent in the waters—presents an image that may well be compared to accounts of the Goddess among the Semites, e.g. Atargatis, Asherah and Tiamat, as well as the Sumerian images of the Goddess as Nina and Nammu." (89)

On that note, I'll share some words from Tikva Frymer-Kensy, author of *In the Wake of the Goddesses*. Tikva notes, "Enki's mother Nammu was mistress of the watery deeps, the Sumerian prototype of the later Tiamat of the Enuma Elish." (71) On Tiamat, she says, "...Ti'amat, the primordial mother, 'she who gave birth to all." (74) Over the years, in my studies, I have read that goddesses were referenced in the Bible in the creation story of Genesis. For example:

"And the earth was without form, and void; and darkness was upon the face of **the deep**. And the Spirit of God moved upon the face of **the waters**." (Genesis 1:2)

That primordial, chaotic abyss of waters that is found in Genesis 1:2 is said to represent the goddess. The watery depths are also analogous to the grave, the pit, and the tomb. All metaphors for the womb of the earth. The beast rising out of the sea can be a metaphor for a king being born. His mother, of course, would be the Dragon (that adulteress who rides the beast).

There are many examples to be found in the Bible of women who embodied the spirit of Babylon. Namely Jezebel, Athaliah, Vashti, Delilah, Herodias and her daughter; these women were rebellious, ambitious, seductive, and ruthless. They sought either the throne or the destruction of the men of God. The modus operandi of the serpent is perfectly encapsulated in their stories. Of those names, Vashti might be the lesser known. I'll briefly summarize how this woman who became a feminist icon serves as a type and shadow of the serpent. As seen in the book of Esther, Queen Vashti refused to come at the King's summon to present her before an audience so that they could behold Vashti's beauty. Her rebellion threatened to inspire rebellion in other women in the kingdom.

"For this deed of the queen shall come abroad unto all women, so that they shall despise their husbands in their eyes, when it shall be reported, The king Ahasuerus commanded Vashti the queen to be brought in before him, but she came not. Likewise shall the ladies of Persia and Media say this day unto all the king's princes, which have heard of the deed of the queen. Thus shall there arise too much contempt and wrath." (Esther 1:17-18)

And so the King decreed that Vashti would never be allowed to come before him again and that her royal estate would be given to a new bride that he would seek out. Had the King not taken a strong stance against the spirit of Babylon in Vashti, his kingdom could have been divided. In Proverbs 7:10-27, King Solomon pleads with the reader to not be seduced by her, and he gives the example of a man who he witnessed to be ensnared by her. There is furthermore a prophetic connection to the words of the Messiah, Jesus Christ, to be found there:

"behold, there met him a woman with the attire of an harlot, and <u>subtil of heart</u>. (She is loud and stubborn; <u>her feet abide not in her house</u>: Now is she without, now in the streets, and <u>lieth in wait</u> at every corner.) So she caught him, and kissed him, and with an impudent face said unto him, I have peace offerings with me; this day have I payed my vows... Come, let us take our fill of love until the morning: let us solace ourselves with loves. For **the goodman is not at home, he is gone a long journey**: He hath taken a bag of money with him, and **will come home at the day appointed**." (Proverbs 7:10-19)

This story becomes a prophetic warning. Keep in mind what the spirit of whoredoms said to the young man to lure him into her clutches. In Mark 13:33-35, Jesus Christ makes a reference to this proverb, saying:

"Take ye heed, watch and pray: **for ye know not when the time is**. For the Son of man is as **a man taking a far journey**, who left his house, and gave authority to his servants, and to every man his work, and commanded the porter to watch. **Watch ye therefore: for ye know not when the master of the house cometh**" (Matthew 13:33-35)

Thus, to reiterate these consequential passages, we see that the Lord describes himself as "a man taking a far journey, who left his house", and the strange woman invites you to take your fill of love with her in his absence. Alas, Jesus Christ warned us not to succumb to her advance. Continuing in Proverbs chapter 7:

"With her much fair speech she caused him to yield, with the flattering of her lips she forced him. He goeth after her straightway, as an ox goeth to the slaughter, or as a fool to the correction of the stocks; Till a dart strike through his liver; as a bird hasteth to the snare, and knoweth not that it is for his life. Hearken unto me now therefore, O ye children, and attend to the words of my mouth. Let not thine heart decline to her ways, go not astray in her paths. For she hath cast down many wounded: yea, **many strong men have been slain by her**. Her house is the way to hell, going down to the chambers of death." (Proverbs 7:19-27)

Another corresponding prophetic message is found in Proverbs chapter 5:

"For the lips of a strange woman drop as an honeycomb, and her mouth is smoother than oil: But her end is bitter as wormwood, **sharp as a twoedged sword**. Her feet go down to death; her steps take hold on hell. Lest thou shouldest ponder the path of life, her ways are moveable, that thou canst not know them. Hear me now therefore, O ye children, and depart not from the words of my mouth. Remove thy way far from her, and come not nigh the door of her house:" (Proverbs 5:3-8)

There is a particular line in this passage that warrants special emphasis. I will break the passage into two parts and discuss each in turn. The first part are the words, "her mouth is smoother than oil: But her end is bitter as wormwood." This is profound and significant prophetic language. When I think of oil, I think of a lamp. Remember the parable of the ten virgins. Five were wise and took oil for their lamps. Five were unwise and took no oil for their lamps. This once again brings us back to the comparison of the two types of women.

Let us consider the meaning of the lamp into which the oil is poured. The lamp is meant to give light which allows men to see. Recall that Proverbs 6:23-24 proclaims, "For the commandment is a lamp; and the law is light; and reproofs of instruction are the way of life: **To keep thee from the evil woman**, from the flattery of the tongue of a strange woman."

This strange woman whose "lips are smoother than oil" is thus a false lamp. Indeed, she gives false light. She seduces men away from the true light of Yah's commandments. And her end is bitter as wormwood. But alas, the identification of this woman as Lucifer, and as a burning lamp does not end there. Revelation 8:10-11 says, "...there fell **a great star** from heaven, burning as it were a lamp, and it fell upon the third part of the rivers, and upon the fountains of waters; And the name of the star is called Wormwood: and the third part of the waters became wormwood; and many men died of the waters, because they were made bitter."

It's worth mentioning here that Mary's name in Hebrew (MARYAM) can mean two things: rebellion and bitter sea. First, Mary's name simply means "rebellion". MAR means "bitter" and YAM means "sea". So, the second meaning of her name could be interpreted as "bitter sea". I see clearly that the strange woman is the fallen star and false light called Wormwood who poisons the waters (representing people) on earth, making them bitter with her false spirit and demonic doctrine.

The other part of the passage which I will examine is that, as Proverbs 3:4 says, the lips of a strange woman are "sharp as a twoedged sword." Hebrews 4:12 proclaims, "For the word of God is quick, and powerful, and **sharper** than any twoedged sword..."

There is a comparison being made: the word of God is sharper than the lips of a strange woman. Revelation 1:16 says of Jesus Christ, "...out of his mouth went a sharp twoedged sword." We know that out of Jesus Christ's mouth went the *"word of God."* In Revelation 2:12-13, Jesus Christ addresses the church in Pergamum, and he says something that's very interesting, in light of this comparison being made; it says, "And to the angel of the church in Pergamos write; These things saith he which hath **the sharp sword with two edges**; I know thy works, and where thou dwellest, even <u>where Satan's seat is</u>."

Jesus Christ made it known that he has the "sharp sword with two edges." Pergamum is where he said Satan's seat was. And Pergamum is where the BLACK ROCK, which was worshiped as the THRONE of the goddess, was once venerated. This goddess is the "strange woman" who we were warned had lips that were "sharp as a twoedged sword".

Figure 10-0-4: The "Lust" tarot card depicting the Great Whore of Babylon.

Figure 10-0-5: "Philosophy" from Universal dictionary of arts, sciences, and literature.

CHAPTER 11: THE MYSTERY OF INIQUITY

There are several key and vital details to be found in Thessalonians 2:1-10 with regard to the adversary that are far too often overlooked. Let us take some time to extract those details because doing so will help to facilitate a correct understanding of the book of Revelation as well. Reading from Thessalonians:

> "Now we beseech you, brethren, by the coming of our Lord Jesus Christ, and by our gathering together unto him, That ye be not soon shaken in mind, or be troubled, neither by spirit, nor by word, nor by letter as from us, as that the day of Christ is at hand. Let no man deceive you by any means: for that day shall not come, except there come a falling away first, and that man of sin be revealed, the son of perdition; Who opposeth and exalteth himself above all that is called God, or that is worshipped; so that he as God sitteth in the temple of God, shewing himself that he is God.
>
> Remember ye not, that, when I was yet with you, I told you these things? And now ye know what withholdeth that he might be revealed in his time. For the **mystery of iniquity** doth already work: only he who now letteth will let, until he be taken out of the way. And then shall that Wicked be revealed, whom the Lord shall consume with the spirit of his mouth, and shall destroy with the brightness of his coming: Even him, whose coming is after the working of Satan with all power and signs and lying wonders, And with all deceivableness of unrighteousness in them that perish; because they received not the love of the truth, that they might be saved." (2 Thessalonians 2:1-10)

The Mystery of Iniquity, as the Apostle Paul said, is working to reveal the son of perdition (the "antichrist"). According to *Blue Letter Bible*, the word "MYSTERY," used in 2 Thessalonians 2:7, comes from mystērion (Strong's G3466). It is derivative of mýō, meaning to shut the mouth. Mystērion is defined as: "a secret or 'mystery' (through the idea of silence imposed by initiation into religious rites):—mystery." The same word is used in the name on the head of the Great Whore of Babylon:

"And upon her forehead was a name written, **MYSTERY**, BABYLON THE GREAT, THE MOTHER OF HARLOTS AND ABOMINATIONS OF THE EARTH." (Revelation 17:5)

"INIQUITY," as it is used in 2 Thessalonians, is anomía (Strong's G458). That is defined as, "illegality, i.e. violation of law or (genitive case) **wickedness**:— iniquity, transgress(-ion of) the law, unrighteousness." I believe that this Mystery of Iniquity, or Mystery of Wickedness, is "MYSTERY, Babylon", the woman riding the beast. Can I prove this theory? Yes, I can! It really is a simple matter, by the grace of the Most High who grants us understanding, of course. Think back to that mysterious woman in Zechariah 5:7-8 who was "sitting inside the basket" and about whom the angel proclaimed "This is Wickedness". Note well that the angel speaking with Zechariah thus defined this woman as the personification of **WICKEDNESS**. Recall also that this woman was carried off by two spirits to the land of Shinar, which is **BABYLON.**

What we have here is a woman who is called wickedness, who dwells in Babylon, and has the name MYSTERY on her forehead. Does that not definitively answer the question of whom *"The Mystery of Iniquity"* is? It is the Great Whore of Babylon! In 2 Thessalonians 2:7, we are told that it was the Mystery of Iniquity which was working to reveal the son of perdition. And then in verse 9, the Apostle Paul uses a different name for the power that is working: Satan.

"For the **mystery of iniquity** doth already <u>work</u>... And then shall that Wicked be revealed... whose coming is after the <u>working</u> of **Satan**..." (2 Thessalonians 2:7-9)

In previous chapters, I explained the significance of the names "mother of harlots" and "mother of abominations" which identify the Queen of Heaven. Now I will focus on the first name that is written on her forehead—MYSTERY. This name is significant because the Mystery cults and secret societies continue the goddess religion in secrecy; or, at least, in a way that is not easy for people to discern. But the signs are all around us in corporate or brand logos, the entertainment industry, and even in the Christian churches themselves. Indeed, the goddess religion never went away, it merely transformed into "Christianity." The authors of *Queen of Rome, Queen of Islam, Queen of All* remark on the Madonna's similarity to other goddesses throughout history:

> "Could the apparitional Queen who is appearing in our day, be the final and ultimate manifestation of Kwanon, Kwan-yin, and a host of other historic goddesses? Will future manifestations of the Queen of Heaven convince the people of the East that she is the ultimate Mother of Mercy? Will this lead to unity under the Queen?... 'Those who know only the Christian tradition do not know how deep the roots of Mary go or how the prayers to her echo the immemorial prayers to ancient goddesses.

The words echo the greeting addressed four thousand years ago to the goddesses Inanna, Ishtar, and Isis as Queen — **Hail! Great Lady of Heaven! Light of the World!**" (45)

When we speak of the Mystery of Iniquity and the Mystery Religions, we're actually talking about the practice of the goddess religion. In the Mystery religions, it is the mother goddess who man must go through for spiritual ascension. Catholicism is a goddess religion. Mary is the "Mother of the Church." Mary becomes Jacob's ladder; she is the mediator between God and man. She births the light, or the child (the sun in the sky and the divine son on the earth). Indeed, in the Mystery religions, when it comes to levels of importance, it is not the son who is key, it is the mother who gives birth to the son who is key. It is the male god who dies, and it is the goddess's role to rebirth (or resurrect) him.

The Mystery religions perpetuate the worship of Lucifer as the supreme goddess through the rituals and symbols that have survived via discrete incorporation into various religions. This concealment of the mysteries was necessary because Rome outwardly condemned paganism (even as it cryptically encoded the pagan theology into its own institutionalized religion). Indeed, virtually every religion has two faces: an exoteric face and an esoteric face. The rituals and symbols that are able to be understood on the surface constitute the exoteric face. But the esoteric face is hidden. Indeed, there are extensive doctrines within religions that are known to exist only by those who have been initiated into the pagan mysteries.

Helena Blavatsky writes about the practices of those initiated ones who come together within secret societies in her two-volume series *Isis Unveiled*:

"They have the relics of what was once a grand form of **nature-worship**, which has been contracted under a despotism into <u>a secret order, hidden from the light of day</u>, and exposed only in the smoky glare of a few burning lamps, in some damp cave or chapel under ground." (402)

While the various "pagan" forms of the goddess religion were outwardly condemned by the Roman empire, through Catholicism it was allowed to exist openly. The devotion to the Divine Feminine was sanctified via concealment within a Christian veneer. To the outsider, the goddess was Mary. To the initiated, she was also Mary—but they knew that Mary was also Lucifer. Even in spite of blasphemous and blatantly pagan titles such as the Queen of Heaven and Mother of God, it never occurred to many Christians over the centuries that they were actually worshiping the Great Whore of Babylon.

Figure 11-0-1: "The Creation of Adam" by Michelangelo shows "God" with his arm wrapped around a mysterious woman.

Even among the Judeans in Christ's day, there were those who worshiped the goddess. Jesus Christ himself had to shut down an attempt made by one woman to exalt his earthly mother above that which is appropriate. As we read in Luke 11:27-28: "And it came to pass, as he spake these things, a certain woman of the company lifted up her voice, and said unto him, **Blessed is the womb** that bare thee, and the paps which thou hast sucked. But he said, <u>Yea rather, blessed are they that hear the word of God, and keep it</u>."

Just as the Messiah said, it's not his mother who is blessed, it's those who hear the word of God and keep it who are blessed. Catholics have made a goddess out of Mary and put her on a pedestal next to Jesus Christ. The titles of Mother of God and Queen of Heaven belong to Lucifer, not to Mary the human mother of Jesus. In fact, Jesus's relation to his mother has absolutely no consequence on our salvation.

In 2 Corinthians 5:15-16, the Apostle Paul says, "...he died for all, that they which live should not henceforth live unto themselves, but unto him which died for them, and rose again. Wherefore henceforth know we no man after the flesh: yea, though we have known Christ after the flesh, yet now henceforth know we him no more."

We no longer know Jesus Christ after the flesh. He is not, "the son of Mary" or the "son of Joseph." He is the Son of God, the risen savior. And, in his own words, he is the ONLY way to the Father in Heaven. In John 1:51, he reveals that he is the ladder that Jacob saw in his dream. That verse reads, "And he saith unto him, Verily, verily, I say unto you, Hereafter ye shall see heaven open, and the angels of God <u>ascending and descending upon **the Son of man**</u>."

He is the bridge between Heaven and earth. He is our one mediator. As 1 Timothy 2:5 says, "For there is one God, and one mediator between God and men, the man Christ Jesus." In John 14:6, Jesus says, "I am the way, the truth, and the life: no man cometh unto the Father, but by me."

These scriptures entirely contradict the Catholic doctrine concerning the role that Mary supposedly plays in the lives of Christians. The Bible clearly says that Jesus Christ is our only savior, mediator, and path to the Father. I'm well aware that some will insist that Mary gets some kind of special treatment because she is supposedly the "Queen Mother" now. But listen to what Jesus says in Matthew 12:46-50:

"While he yet talked to the people, behold, his mother and his brethren stood without, desiring to speak with him. Then one said unto him, Behold, thy mother and thy brethren stand without, desiring to speak with thee. But he answered and said unto him that told him, Who is my mother? and who are my brethren? And he stretched forth his hand **toward his disciples**, and said, Behold my mother and my brethren! <u>For whosoever shall do the will of my Father which is in heaven, the same is my brother, and sister, and **mother**</u>." (Matthew 12:46-50)

That's it. Whoever does the will of his Father which is in heaven is Jesus's brother, sister, and mother. Mary gets no special treatment. End of story.

Figure 11-0-2: "Virgo" by Sidney Hall (1825), restored by Adam Cuerden.

CHAPTER 12: THE SUN OF PERDITION

The image of the mother goddess and her son has endured throughout the ages, being carried from kingdom to kingdom. Where did this image come from? Or, in other words, what was its origin?

Figure 12-0-1: The "Mother of God" at Hagia Sophia (via World History Encyclopedia).

To understand, you only need to look up at the constellation of Virgo. Mark Stavish, the author of *Freemasonry: Rituals, Symbols & History of the Secret Society*, writes, "the key part to consider in relation to sacred geometry is the first: 'That which is above is as that which is below, and that which is below is as that which is above." (90)

The virgin and her son are seen in the sky every September, when the sun is positioned in the constellation of Virgo. The sign meant to represent the righteous woman, Israel, has been taken by the Whore of Babylon to represent herself. The Mystery of Iniquity is so pervasive, in fact, that nearly everything we can point to in corporate logos or in entertainment somehow points to the worship of Virgo, Venus, or her sun.

What does her sun represent? The answer is: God. But it's not the "God" outside, it's the "god" inside. **The sun represents the divine light that is within man**. When the sun god Osiris is resurrected by Isis, he is rebirthed as her son Horus. This is a metaphor for the raising of the "god" within man that is currently "dead," lost in the darkness of the flesh prison and ignorance, waiting to be resurrected by Isis (the Mother of the Mysteries).

As said in *The Secret Doctrine, Volume I*, by H. P. Blavatksy, "The 'Son' of the immaculate Celestial Virgin... is born again on Earth as the Son of the terrestrial Eve—our mother Earth, and becomes Humanity as a total—past, present, and future... Above, the Son is the whole Kosmos; below, he is Mankind." (60)

The divine light, the divine spark, or the Christ within, according to the Mystery religions, is an energy that is inside and throughout everything that exists. It is in the trees, the water, the rocks, people, and so on. It's known by many names: the Force, the ONE, Brahma, Ain Soph, the Universal Consciousness, the great Mind of the universe, and just plain "God." From this point on, I will refer to this Mystery religion "God" as "the Force."

If the Force is in nature, then NATURE is "God." People of reprobate minds have "changed the truth of God into a lie, and worshipped and served the creature more than the Creator, who is blessed for ever." (Romans 1:25) Unlike the Force, the true God, Yahawah, is not in all His creation. The Bible tells us plainly, in several places, that not all have the Spirit of Yah in them:

"And we are his witnesses of these things; and so is also the Holy Ghost, whom God hath given to them that obey him" (Acts 5:23)

"But ye are not in the flesh, but in the Spirit, if so be that the Spirit of God dwell in you." (Romans 8:9)

"And I will pray the Father, and he shall give you another Comforter, that he may abide with you for ever; Even the Spirit of truth; whom the world cannot receive, because it seeth him not, neither knoweth him: but ye know him; for he dwelleth with you, and shall be in you." (John 14:16-17)

This is a big difference between the true Creator (Yahawah) and the Mystery god. "The Force" is what I believe the Higgs Boson, or the so-called "god particle," truly refers to. The scientists at CERN claim to have already discovered this "field". On CERN's website page on the Higgs Boson, it says, "You and everything around you are made of particles. But when the universe began, no particles had mass; they all sped around at the speed of light. Stars, planets and life could only emerge because particles gained their mass from a fundamental field associated with the Higgs boson. The existence of this mass-giving field was confirmed in 2012, when the Higgs boson particle was discovered at CERN."

A field that permeates everything? That's the Force. Science, falsely-so-called, seems to be blurring the lines between itself and spirituality more than people like to admit. Maybe that should not be surprising considering that the Greek word used for "science" in 1 Timothy 6:20 is GNOSIS (G1097).

"O Timothy, keep that which is committed to thy trust, avoiding profane and vain babblings, and oppositions of **science** falsely so called:" (1 Timothy 6:20)

In the *Blue Letter Bible*, gnosis is defined as: "knowing (the act), i.e. (by implication) knowledge." As I have seen it described, gnosis is gaining an intimate experience with, or understanding of, who or what "God" is without having to be told who or what "God" is.

For those of us who believe the Bible, it's worth noting that the Hindu god Shiva is called "the destroyer," and he destroys the old age to prepare the way for the new. The Beast which ascends out from the bottomless pit is called "Apollyon" and "Abaddon," both names which mean "destroyer." Revelation 17:8 says that the Beast shall ascend out of the bottomless pit and "go into perdition." The word perdition means destruction. I think it's safe to say that Shiva represents the son of perdition, also known as the anti-christ and the Beast. This relates to CERN, because a prominent statue of Shiva has been erected in the courtyard of the CERN facility. Another fascinating connection is with regard to the god Cernunnos, also called the "Green Man". Cernunnos is yet another deity who shares a consort-type relationship with the goddess. One can't help but take notice of the similarity between the names of CERN and Cernunnos.

The consort of the goddess is often associated with the sun and/or animal life. Because the Sun rises and sets, and creatures live and die, the consort of the goddess goes through a cycle of death and resurrection. In Revelation 17:8, the angel talking with John says of the Beast which ascends out of the bottomless pit: "The beast that thou sawest was, and is not; and shall ascend out of the bottomless pit, and go into perdition: and they that dwell on the earth shall wonder, whose names were not written in the book of life from the foundation of the world, when they behold the beast that was, and is not, and yet is."

This prophecy distinguishes the true Christ from the "anti-christ." While the anti-christ "was, and is not, and yet is," (Revelation 17:8) the true Christ is he "... which is, and which was, and which is to come." (Revelation 1:4) This means that even though Jesus Christ subjected himself to death, he never ceased to be.

As I said at the start of this chapter, the expression, "as above, so below" describes how—in the mystery religions—the sun represents the light of the divine within man. The rising sun is a metaphor for enlightenment and spiritual ascension. It's the resurrection of the dead god within, so that his or her light can shine. In Freemasonry, this is the raising of the slain builder (Hiram Abiff); his casket is sometimes seen in Masonic art. This symbolism of the sun is why the "rising sun" is the symbol of the Master Mason.

Understanding this, the title of "the Beast who was, and is not, and yet is" is significant because it literally speaks of someone who is raised from the dead, and it spiritually speaks of someone who is enlightened through the Mystery religions. When people talk about the Christ within, becoming Christs, or the Christ consciousness, they are speaking of that anti-christ "divine spark." It is a false light, and they are false Christs.

The apostle Paul says in 2 Corinthians 11:3-4, "But I fear, lest by any means, as the serpent beguiled Eve through his subtilty, so your minds should be corrupted from the simplicity that is in Christ. For if he that cometh preacheth another Jesus, whom we have not preached, or if ye receive another spirit, which ye have not received, or another gospel, which ye have not accepted, ye might well bear with him."

This is so important because I see so many believers in the Bible being deceived by Gnostics and Luciferians claiming to be sent by the Most High God, Yah. But the Jesus that they bring to you is not the same as this Jesus that is in the Bible. As the prophet says in the book of Isaiah: "To the law and to the testimony: if they speak not according to this word, it is because there is no light in them." (Isaiah 8:20)

The "Jesus Christ" that the Luciferians speak of is not the one that is described in the testimony that the disciple John gave:

"In the beginning was the Word, and the Word was with God, and the Word was God. The same was in the beginning with God. All things were made by him; and without him was not any thing made that was made. In him was life; and the life was the light of men. And the light shineth in darkness; and the darkness comprehended it not."

"That was the true Light, which lighteth every man that cometh into the world. He was in the world, and the world was made by him, and the world knew him not. He came unto his own, and his own received him not. But as many as received him, to them gave he power to become the sons of God, even to them that believe on his name: Which were born, not of blood, nor of the will of the flesh, nor of the will of man, but of God. And the Word was made flesh, and dwelt among us, (and we beheld his glory, the glory as of the only begotten of the Father,) full of grace and truth." (John 1:1-5, 9-14)

Some don't want to believe what the Bible says about ALL THINGS being made by Jesus Christ (Yahawashai). Some still want their Luciferian, gnostic lies about the world and man being made by an evil creator. They want to believe that the god of the old testament (YHWH) is actually "Satan"; the Gnostics call him the Demiurge. Those people want another Jesus. I strongly advise you to run far from any doctrine that comes from the Nag Hammadi texts. There is NO truth in the "gnostic gospels." Learn who the true Jesus Christ is according to the scriptures and accept HIM for your salvation:

"Moreover, brethren, I declare unto you the gospel which I preached unto you, which also ye have received, and wherein ye stand; By which also ye are saved, if ye keep in memory what I preached unto you, unless ye have believed in vain. For I delivered unto you first of all that which I also received, how that Christ died for our sins according to the scriptures; And that he was buried, and that he rose again the third day according to the scriptures" (1 Corinthians 15:1-4)

You need a savior. You cannot save yourself. Understand this and believe that Jesus Christ rose physically and literally from the dead. As the apostle Paul says, "The word is nigh thee, even in thy mouth, and in thy heart: that is, the word of faith, which we preach; That if thou shalt confess with thy mouth the Lord Jesus, and shalt believe in thine heart that God hath raised him from the dead, thou shalt be saved." (Romans 10:8-9) Once you have believed, turn from your sins and ask our Father in Heaven to give you the strength to resist sin.

"Shall we continue in sin, that grace may abound? God forbid. How shall we, that are dead to sin, live any longer therein?... Let not sin therefore reign in your mortal body, that ye should obey it in the lusts thereof. Neither yield ye your members as instruments of unrighteousness unto sin: but yield yourselves unto God, as those that are alive from the dead, and your members as instruments of righteousness unto God." (Romans 6:1-2, 12-13)

Figure 12-0-2: The Widow (Isis) weeps over a broken pillar representing her dead husband (the sun).

CHAPTER 13: MOTHER OF HARLOTS & ABOMINATIONS

The "Great Goddess" represents rebellion against everything that the Most High God Yah stands for. The number 13 also represents rebellion and follows her. Nimrod was of the 13th generation from Adam and his kingdom began at BABYLON. There were 12 disciples with Jesus Christ at the last supper, and the Devil was among them. The name on the forehead of the woman riding the beast (MYSTERY, BABYLON THE GREAT, THE MOTHER OF HARLOTS AND ABOMINATIONS OF THE EARTH) has 13 words.

The link between the goddess and the number 13 goes deep. As Monica Sjoo and Barbara Mor, the authors of *The Great Cosmic Mother: Rediscovering the Religion of the Earth,* detail:

"On December 13, in Sweden, **St. Lucia** travels in procession as the **Queen of Light**, with a crown of candles in her hair, surrounded by her maidens.... The Festival of the Greek Hecate on August 13th. Thirteen members in a witch coven... Among pagan Scandinavians Friday the 13th was celebrated as a beneficent day; Friday is Freya/Frigga's day... and thirteen is the number of lunar months in a year. Many Patriarchal 'bad omens' are simply reversals of what was sacred to matriarchy and the Goddess religion." (156-157)

Figure 13-0-1: A Saint Lucy's Day procession on December 13 (photo by Claudia Gründer).

The letter M is the 13th letter of the alphabet and, as Barbara G. Walker puts forth, "The letter M seems to have been based on symbols of the twin peaks of the holy mountain, which were often seen as breasts of the Great Mother." (346) Upside down, the letter M becomes a W and resembles the Hebrew letter SHIN which is the first letter in the name of Shekinah, the feminine aspect of "God" in Judaism.

Figure 13-0-2: Virgo astrological sign.

The letter M is also the sign of both the constellations of Virgo and Scorpio. Demetra George and Douglas Bloch, authors of *Asteroid Goddesses*, explains some of the connections between them, stating, "In the original zodiacal belt outlined by the Assyrian and Babylonian cultures, Scorpio was symbolized by a serpent and directly followed the sign Virgo... The Virgo and Scorpio glyphs were similar in design but contained subtle distinctions." (124)

The letter M also represents Mary, or the Madonna. Michelangelo's famous Madonna della Pietà statue has the letter M designed into Mary's left hand. Her right hand is making either an M or a W sign. And, as mentioned before, the name Mary means "REBELLION," so that perfectly fits the number 13.

Like the authors Monica Sjoo and Barbara Mor said, what we associate with bad omens are apparently "reversals of **what was sacred to matriarchy and the Goddess religion**." The titles of the mother goddess, such as the "mother of harlots" and the "mother of the gods" are branded on the head of the Great Whore of Babylon like a label of infamy. Throughout human history, it was HER who corrupted the earth with her sorceries and debaucherous religion. All religion apart from the truth of YAH **will** lead to the goddess Lucy.

As explained in previous chapters, evidence from the paleolithic and neolithic eras shows that the religion of the pre-flood world was centered on the worship of the nature and fertility goddess. This religion probably survived the flood either by some of Noah's sons or their wives. The dying and resurrecting gods, often represented by the sun, vegetation and wildlife (such as deer and bulls), first appeared in Mesopotamia. We also see the rise of male father gods who become the "king of the gods" as counterfeits to the Most High God, Yah. These sky fathers and kings of the gods, such as Marduk, Odin and Zeus and so on, were the authority figures and reflected a shift to patriarchal culture in general. Meanwhile Lucifer presented herself as his wife and/or mother.

Even with a shift towards patriarchy in society, the goddess still maintained a firm grasp on her power, as explained by Merlin Stone:

"**In Mesopotamia, the goddess is supreme**,' wrote Professor Henri Frankfort in his 1948 publication of *Kingship and the Gods* 'because the source of all life is seen as female. Hence the god descends from her and is called her son, though he is also her husband. In the ritual of the sacred marriage, the goddess holds the initiative throughout. Even in the condition of chaos, the female Tiamat is the leader and Apsu is merely her male complement." (26)

Alan Butler writes the following, in *America Nation of the Goddess*, about the eternal nature of the goddess in the Mystery religions: "In all the ancient Mystery religions the god is constantly born and dies, while the Goddess is eternal..." (99) The reason, as he explains, is "Because nature itself was synonymous with the Goddess of the Mystery rites, the Goddess herself was seen as being eternal, whereas her consort, who was also her son and was represented by the barley, died and was reborn each year." (183)

Merlin Stone observes, "...**wherever this dying young consort appears as the male deity, we may recognize the presence of the religion of the Goddess**, the legends and lamentation rituals of which are extraordinarily similar in so many cultures." (19)

As you can find in Masonic art or statues, there is a woman who weeps over a broken pillar (or over a grave). The broken pillar represents her dead son or husband who must be resurrected or rebirthed by her. This woman is Isis, the Widow. She mourns for her fallen son/lover. Father Time stands behind her, braiding her hair that was purposefully made disheveled by the woman when she went into mourning. The braiding of her hair represents the healing of her wounds and the end of her mourning period. We can also see her in the form of the Virgin Mary, weeping over the body of her dead son.

Figure 13-0-3: Michelangelo's "Pieta" glorifies Lucifer as the eternal mother while Jesus Christ appears defeated.

Unfortunately, the origin of this repeating image of the goddess and her dying son has been attributed to the easily debunked myth of Semiramis being the mother of Tammuz and the wife of Nimrod. That disinformation has caused people to stop looking for the truth behind the image. The truth is that this woman is the spirit of "MYSTERY, Babylon." And since the Most High overthrew the pre-flood world, Lucifer has had to rebrand herself as the "Mother of God" and the "wife of YAH" to gain worship among His people.

Manly P. Hall explains the connections that Venus has to the sun in *The Secret Teachings of All Ages*:

"As the morning star, **Venus** is visible before sunrise, and as the evening star it shines forth immediately after the sunset. Because of these qualities, a number of names have been given to it by the ancients. Being visible in the sky at sunset, it was called vesper, and as it arose before the sun, it was called the false light, the star of the morning, or **Lucifer**, which means the light-bearer. Because of this relation to the sun, the planet was also referred to as Venus, Astarte, Aphrodite, Isis, and **The Mother of the Gods**." (204)

Figure 13-0-4: The astrological sign for Virgo at the Wisconsin State Capitol.

One of the goddesses that was worshiped as the Mother of the Gods was Asherah. And—somehow—she was able to convince the ancient Israelites that she was the "wife of Yahweh." In the book, *Reinstating the Divine Woman in Judaism*, Jenny Kien offers some key details about this mother goddess:

"The first millennium BCE brought further changes to Phoenician religion. Asherah disappeared, to be replaced by Tannit, a name derived from one of her epithets meaning **Serpent Lady**. She also seems to have lost her role as Queen of the Whole Heavens, being reduced to a lunar goddess. In Carthage a transcendent Ba'alshamem dominated the pantheon, and Tannit became Phaneba'al, the face of Ba'al. In other words, in this millennium, Asherah, the great goddess, had become the presence of Ba'al much as the female Shekinah of the Kabbalah is said to represent the presence of Jahweh." (59)

Asherah was called the "**Serpent Lady**." That old serpent claimed to be the wife of the Most High God. John Day says of this mother goddess in his book, *Yahweh and the Gods and Goddesses of Canaan*:

"...we have already noted that the mention of 'the host of heaven' alongside Asherah in several Old Testament references may imply her position as mother of the gods; further, with regard to her fertility aspect, it may be noted Athirat is sometimes called Qudshu in the Ugaritic text..., and second-millenium BCE representations of Qudshu (roughly contemporary with the Ugaritic texts) have been found in Egypt that show her to have been a fertility goddess of erotic character..." (48)

As with many other goddesses, fornication is merely a form of worship in Asherah's religion. Jenny Kien gives more information on what Asherah was related to:

"Even more important than the snake, Asherah's major symbol over many, many centuries was **the sacred tree**. Both extra-biblical and biblical evidence and biblical tradition associate Asherah with trees... Her image, the asherah, was wooden and is sometimes referred to as being planted, i.e. a tree, or as something made and set up, such as a carved trunk or pole. There are clear Deuteronomic instructions not to plant any trees or set up asherot next to Jahweh altars." (126)

Throughout the Bible, the enemy of the Most High and His people has been identified as the Serpent. A serpent that originally appeared at the tree of knowledge of good and evil. And when you look at history and at what is in the Bible, what do you see? A goddess who keeps causing a problem among the Israelites, who just happens to be called "Serpent Lady" and worshiped in association with trees. Some of her idols were even trees or images carved out of trees.

Figure 13-0-5: Virgin in the parish church of St. Ulrich in Gröden (photo by Wolfgang Moroder).

As we read in the Bible, the Most High gave commandment against putting images that belonged to the goddess anywhere near His altars or places of worship: "Thou shalt not plant thee a grove of any trees near unto the altar of the LORD thy God, which thou shalt make thee." (Deuteronomy 16:21) What's interesting here is that the Hebrew word for grove (H842) is ASHERAH. So the verse truly says: "Thou shalt not plant thee an ASHERAH of any trees near unto the altar of the LORD thy God, which thou shalt make thee." Once the images of the Queen of Heaven are placed in His sanctuary, the Most High will not abide there; then those who worship will be left worshiping only Lucifer and her counterfeit "God."

Even the Jewish Rabbis of modern times have given the goddess a place in Judaism as the "Shekinah glory." You may notice that the name Shekinah is not in your Bibles, but you'll see religious people refer to Shekinah as the "glory of god" or even the holy spirit. They are all wrong. This is just another form of Lucifer who creeps her way into any place where the Most High is being worshipped. The same thing goes for Sophia. She's not the Holy Spirit, she is the spirit of whoredoms. The authors of *The Cosmic Shekinah*, Sorita d'Este and David Rankine, draw a connection between Shekinah and Asherah:

"The relationship between the Shekinah and **the serpent** is significant, particularly in light of the ambivalent nature of the symbolism associated with serpents in different cultures. Considering other **wisdom goddesses**, the serpent motif recurs with a number of them. For instance the Canaanite wisdom and mother goddess Asherah was known as the lady of the serpent." (22)

This serpent goddess is constantly associated with "wisdom," but the Bible draws a clear distinction between the wisdom of the world (Sophia, Isis, and Athena) and the wisdom of Yahawah. The Bible also says that Jesus Christ was made wisdom for those who believe on him (1 Corinthians 1:30). Those under the influence of the "devilish" Sophia exhibit her sinful characteristics, and are not "wise" at all, but foolish. The Bible gives us a several admonishments not to follow the world's "wisdom":

"...hath not God made foolish **the wisdom of this world**? " (1 Corinthians 1:20)

"For the wisdom of this world is foolishness with God..." (1 Corinthians 3:19)

"This wisdom descendeth not from above, but is earthly, sensual, **devilish**." (James 3:15)

Remember that I said there was a seed-war between the "wise woman" and the "foolish woman;" Lucifer claims to be the Goddess of Wisdom. It's fascinating that the apostle Paul called the wisdom (Sophia) of the world FOOLISH. Abraham Cohen, the author of *Everyman's Talmud: The Major Teachings of Rabbinic Sages*, reveals the way that Judaism has reinstated the wisdom goddess under the identity of Shekinah:

> "...the Shechinah is often depicted under the figure of light. The Scriptural phrase, 'The earth did shine with His glory' (Ezek. xliii. 2), receives the comment, 'This is the face of the Shechinah' (ARN II); and the priestly benediction, 'The Lord make His face to shine upon thee' (Num. vi 25) is interpreted, 'May He give thee the light of the Shechinah' (Num. R. xi. 5)." (42)

> "Sufficient has been quoted to demonstrate how untenable is the view that the Talmudic conception of God is wholly transcendental. However reluctant the teachers of Israel were to identify God with His Universe and insisted on His being exalted high above the abode of men, yet they thought of **the world as permeated through and through with the omnipresent Shechinah**. God is at once above the Universe and the very soul of the Universe." (47)

DeAnne Loper, author of *Kabbalah Secrets Christians Need to Know*, shares information on the creation of the "divine sparks" that came from the EIN SOPH (who is the Kabbalistic version of "the Force"):

> "The kabbalists say that in order to make room for creation, Ein Soph had to contract himself to a single point, making room for the worlds of the Sefirot... but the vessels could not contain the 'divine light" ... As the vessels shattered the light dispersed and scattered in the form of 'sparks.' Some of these sparks rose back up to their 'source.' Others descended, becoming trapped in matter... and because god is in everything and everyone, god himself is in the pit waiting to be released... Into the deep abyss... there fell, as a result of the breaking of the vessels, forces of holiness, **sparks of divine light**. Hence there is a Galut of the divine itself, of the **'sparks of the Shekinah:'** 'These sparks of holiness are bound in fetters of steel in the depths of the shells, and yearningly aspire to rise to their source but cannot avail to do so until they have support." (46-47)

The Rabbis have given "God" a female aspect, allowing him to be both separate from creation as the Ain Soph, and within creation as the Shekinah. In doing so, they are consistent with the Mystery religion doctrine, which has **"God" manifest in the material world in a female form**. Instead of Gaia, Sophia, or Shakti, Judaism has Shekinah. And on that note, I can't help but feel that there is a connection between the names "Shekinah" and "Shakti." Sorita d'Este and David Rankine help us draw further connections between the Jewish goddess and the Hindu goddess:

"In parallel with the Shekinah and her earlier manifestations, there was another goddess being worshipped in another part of the world who manifested through many forms, the Indian Shakti (or Sakti). Shakti means 'power' or 'energy', and she is viewed as the cosmic power or energy which creates change... Like the Shekinah, she has the cosmic or Heavenly manifestation, and also an Earthly manifestation within everyone, **as the kundalini, or serpent fire power**." (120)

In *The Hebrew Goddess*, by Raphael Patai, other names are given for the goddess Shakti who is the spirit in kundalini:

"...Parvati the Great Mother, symbolized by the female generative organ [the Yoni], and known by many other names, among them especially Devi (goddess)... Parvati assumes terrifying forms also, such as that of Kali... She is also known as Shakti ('Power')... Anyone who truly grasps the goddess's complete nature can master the whole universe, **because he becomes one with her**." (121)

There were two ways that a male devotee of the goddess could become "one with her." The first way: he committed fornication with the temple prostitute (the high priestess) who represented the goddess on earth. As I explained previously, when the Bible says that the kings of the earth committed fornication with the Great Whore of Babylon, it was being **literal**. It was required of kings to commit fornication with the representation of the goddess to establish their legitimacy to the throne.

The role of the high priestesses always went to the women, obviously, because they were appropriate for the role of "goddess on earth." It's why we see the knowledge of the Serpent passed down from Eve to Adam, not from Adam to Eve. And these high priestesses were also called prophetesses. Remember that in Revelation 2:20, Jesus Christ said of that woman Jezebel, that she calleth herself a prophetess.

The second way: the male devotee castrated himself and prostituted himself at the goddess's temple. Not only was Babylon the **mother of** female temple **harlots,** but she was the mother of MALE temple prostitutes as well. As many Bible readers may know already, a man which wears that which pertains to a woman is an **abomination** to the Most High God (Deuteronomy 22:5). Yah gave His people commandment in Deuteronomy 23:17: "There shall be no whore of the daughters of Israel, nor a **sodomite** of the sons of Israel."

The word sodomite has usually been applied to gay men in general but looking at it biblically, as it says here in Deuteronomy 23:17, a sodomite (a kadesh) is the male version of a whore (a kadesha). I imagine Sodom had to be overrun with these male temple prostitutes. The next time you see a statue of a goddess that looks like a man, guess what, you're looking at a sodomite.

Figure 13-0-6: Attis, consort of the goddess Kybele. Members of his cult castrated themselves like their god Attis.

Figure 13-0-7: "The Whore of Babylon" by William Blake (1809). Souls are born from the chalice and are eventually devoured by the beast.

CHAPTER 14: RULER OVER THE DARKNESS

"And God said, Let there be light: and there was light. And God saw the light, that it was good: and God divided the light from the darkness. And God called the light Day, **and the darkness he called Night**." (Genesis 1:3-5)

Who is the ruler over the darkness? When put that way, I think most of us can rightly guess the answer: Satan. But if I had said, WHAT is the ruler over the darkness, many people would be at a loss for what to answer. The answer is in the Bible, and we should carefully consider what it implies.

"And God made two great lights; the greater light to rule the day, and the **lesser light to rule the night**..." (Genesis 1:16)

There should be no doubt that the "lesser light" is a reference to the moon. The "greater light" is the sun. That should be obvious. So, the moon rules over the night and over the darkness. I find myself often quoting Ephesians 6:15 which tells us that we are wrestling against spiritual wickedness and against the *"rulers of the darkness of this world."* Having said all of that, it should be clear that the moon can be a representation for Satan... according to scripture! The sun then represents righteousness. It represents all that is good.

"For, behold, the day cometh, that shall burn as an oven; and all the proud, yea, and all that do wickedly, shall be stubble: and the day that cometh shall burn them up, saith the LORD of hosts, that it shall leave them neither root nor branch. But unto you that fear my name shall the Sun of righteousness arise with healing in his wings..." (Malachi 4:1-2)

Understanding that, to be "clothed with the sun" means to have righteousness put on, doesn't it? Revelation 12:1 reads, "And a great sign appeared in heaven: a woman clothed in the sun, with the moon under her feet and a crown of twelve stars on her head." This image describing the constellation of Virgo, and representing Israel, has been declared by the devotees of the goddess to be a representation of their Madonna. Clothed with the sun and standing on the symbols of Satan (the moon and the serpent), Lucifer has been transformed from the "Great Whore of Babylon" to an angel of light called "the Virgin Mary."

Figure 14-0-1: Giovanni Battista Tiepolo's Immaculate Conception (1767–1768).

According to *Online Etymology Dictionary*, the name Madonna comes from old Italian MA DONNA meaning "my lady." I have found her name in the book of Job. In Job 38:31, the Most High Yahawah asks Job, "Canst thou bind the sweet influences of Pleiades, or loose the bands of Orion?" The Hebrew word for "influences" is only found once in the entire Bible. It is ma'ădannâ (Strong's H4575). If we replace "influences" with the Hebrew word, we get: "Canst thou bind the sweet ma'ădannâ of Pleiades". (Job 38:31)

In statues and paintings, it's Madonna who stands on the serpent with the moon beneath her feet, but Genesis 3:15 says that the seed of the woman (who is Jesus Christ) would bruise the head of the serpent. Understanding that the serpent is a symbol for the goddess, it's no wonder that the serpent doesn't appear to be harmed by the goddess standing on it. As the serpent and moon also represent regeneration (or death and rebirth), the goddess standing on them shows her mastery over them. Linda Foubister notes, "The moon undergoes periodic rebirth in the sky every 29 1/2 days, much as the snake undergoes rebirth when it sheds its skin, and women shed menstrual blood in a lunar cycle." (4)

While not every culture regarded the moon as feminine, the Bible does use the moon as a symbol for the mothers of the twelve sons of Jacob/Israel:

"And [Joseph] dreamed yet another dream, and told it his brethren, and said, Behold, I have dreamed a dream more; and, behold, the sun and **the moon** and the eleven stars made obeisance to me. And he told it to his father, and to his brethren: and his father rebuked him, and said unto him, What is this dream that thou hast dreamed? Shall I and **thy mother** and thy brethren indeed come to bow down ourselves to thee to the earth?" (Genesis 37:9-10)

Because of this feminine nature of the moon in the Bible, the association of the moon with goddesses is fitting. Diana Brueton, author of *Many Moons*, lists some of those goddesses: "Isis, Diana, Selene, Helen, Hathor, Artemis... the ancient civilizations created many goddesses whose power and influence came from the Moon. Their essence was that of the Moon itself, with its subtle but vital pull on the forces of life." (53)

Like the apostle Paul said, "those who sleep, sleep in the night." Babylon is the spirit of deep sleep, and she has made all who live in darkness both drunken and blind. As Jeremiah 57:7 says, "Babylon hath been a golden cup in the LORD'S hand, **that made all the earth drunken**: the nations have drunken of her wine; therefore the nations are mad." It's not literal wine that Babylon makes the world drunk with, as scripture tells us:

"...they are drunken, <u>but not with wine</u>; they stagger, but not with strong drink. For the LORD hath poured out upon you **the SPIRIT of deep sleep**, and hath <u>closed your eyes</u>: the prophets and your rulers, the seers hath he covered." (Isaiah 29:9-10)

The apostle Paul tells us more about Babylon who has made the earth drunken, and who we now know is the "SPIRIT of deep sleep":

"(According as it is written, God hath given them the **SPIRIT** of slumber, <u>eyes that they should not see</u>, and ears that they should not hear;) unto this day." (Romans 11:8)

"But if our gospel be hid, it is hid to them that are lost: In whom **the god of this world** hath <u>blinded the minds of them which believe not</u>, lest the light of the glorious gospel of Christ, who is the image of God, should shine unto them." (2 Corinthians 4:3-4)

"Ye are all the children of light, and the children of the day: we are not of the night, nor **of darkness**. Therefore <u>let us not sleep</u>, as do others; but let us watch and be sober. For they that sleep <u>sleep in the **night**</u>; and they that be drunken <u>are drunken in the **night**</u>." (1 Thessalonians 5:5-7)

The children of darkness are ruled by the Moon Goddess; and they are drunken, asleep, and their minds are blinded. I do not believe that the myth of Lilith is true but I know that her spirit is very real. A creature of the night, the owl, often accompanies "wisdom goddesses" such as Athena (Minerva) and Isis. Since owls are nocturnal that creates a connection with the moon, which might explain why it seems like the owl has always been linked with the Divine Feminine.

It's worth recognizing that the Hebrew word for "screech owl" is **LILIT**, or **LILITH** (Strong's H3917). This word is found only once in the Bible, in the book of Isaiah: "The wild beasts of the desert shall also meet with the wild beasts of the island, and the satyr shall cry to his fellow; the **screech owl** also shall rest there, and find for herself a place of rest." (Isaiah 34:14)

Figure 14-0-2: Winged woman with a pentagram over her head, presumed to be Lilith.

She is the "dark mother" (Kali), also known as the hidden and mysterious "dark matter" of space. "Matter" comes from "mater," meaning mother. The "light" of the Mysteries is born from the darkness of the black mater, or black Madonna. Diana Brueton says of Madonna:

> "Still more notorious and famous to modern man comes Mary the Madonna, one of the supreme examples of Mother Goddess, and as such incorporating many ancient Sun and Moon beliefs. She is turned to for help with childbirth, crop-growing, healing — the traditional nurturing values. **...the moon became more associated with Mary**, and she took on all forms of lunar symbolism and imagery. Pope Innocent III told sinners: 'Towards the Moon it is he should look, who is buried in the shades of sin and iniquity. Having lost grace, the day disappears and there is no more sin for him, but the Moon is still on the horizon. Let him address himself to Mary; under her influence thousands every day find their way to God." (56)

Who is that "moon god" being worshiped in Mecca, really? Haven't we proven that the moon is feminine? The Quran says that Allah does not beget (112:3). To "beget" means to father a child. Yah, the God of the Bible, says He has a "begotten son" (Psalm 2:7). So, Allah and Yah can't be the same God. You know who **can't** beget? A WOMAN.

I don't think it's a coincidence that a well-known Islamic terrorist group is named **ISIS** and that the Great Mosque of Mecca (Masjid al-Haram) is shaped like an Isis knot. In *Arabian Religion Before Muhammad*, Dr. Brian Bradford remarks, in response to Allah being regarded as the Lord of Sirius, "the star which the pagan Arabs used to worship which represented **a female deity**." (55)

The worship of the triple goddess in Arabia is well documented, and I have much more to share about that. Merlin Stone, in *Ancient Mirrors of Womanhood* informs us: "**Al-Uzza**, though most often associated with the planet Venus, was at times described as the star **Sirius**, sacred star of the Egyptian Goddess **Isis**." (123-124)

Figure 14-0-3: An Isis Knot next to an aerial view of Masjid al-Haram.

It's well known that Isis (Sopdet) is the personification of the star Sirius. Venus has also become identified as the goddess of Sirius, which adds up considering that **Al-Uzza was associated with both Venus and Sirius**. Lucifer has patiently bided her time under the disguise of "Allah" out of necessity for many centuries, since the death and resurrection of Jesus Christ truly bruised her head and forced the goddess religion into hiding. But she can't help but reveal herself because she wants to be known; she doesn't want a MALE god getting all the glory. In what name do her worshipers strike fear into the hearts of their enemies? **ISIS**!

What is the true reason the terrorist group ISIS beheads their enemies? The reason is that the spirit of Babylon seeks to usurp authority over men, especially "*the man*," Christ Jesus. Beheading is symbolic of cutting off authority or government (the mind being the part that governs). Isaiah 9:6 says of Christ, "the government shall be upon his shoulder." The apostle Paul made God's order clear when he said, "But I would have you know, that **the head of every man is Christ**; and the head of the woman is the man; and the head of Christ is God." (1 Corinthians 11:3) Lucifer hates the Most High's order, and ISIS's brutal method of beheading represents her hatred for it and her refusal to submit to it.

Figure 14-0-4: "The Fall" by Kenyon Cox (1892).

In the garden of Eden, the Serpent "cut off the head" (the man) and went directly to Eve, making HER the head. Eve, rather than consulting Adam, usurped his authority and ate the fruit. Till this day, Eve is viewed by feminists and occultists as a heroine and a rebel icon. **She was the first avatar of the goddess, the first High Priestess**, and the first person to initiate another (Adam) into the knowledge of good and evil. Her Hebrew name, Chavah (Havah), means "mother of life" or "mother of all living." This too identifies her with the image of the goddess. I believe the word "evil" comes from the name EVE. The end of daylight and the beginning of darkness is the EVE-ening. Venus is both the "light-bearer" and the EVE-ening star.

Venus is also Freya. Friday is Freya's day. Friday is the day of the most important prayer for the Muslim faithful. Freya is a Norse goddess whose equivalent is Kybele of Phrygia (now called Turkey). The same type of black rock (or possibly even the same black rock) being venerated in Mecca at the Kaaba was involved in Kybele's worship. Black stones were also involved in the worship of the pre-Islamic Arabic goddesses (Al-Uzza, Manat, and Al-Lat) which the Qurayish tribe that Muhammad was from were devoted to. The name of the Qurayish tribe, who were the keepers of the Kaaba, is etymologically linked to the goddess Q're (Greek: Kore). *THEOI* gives the following information on Kore:

"...[Persephone] was worshipped alongside her mother Demeter in the Eleusinian Mysteries. This agricultural-based cult promised its initiates passage to a blessed afterlife. Persephone was titled Kore (Core) (the Maiden)."

There's no doubt that the stone in the Kaaba belongs to Al-Uzza. Francis E. Peters, author of *Mecca: A Literary History of the Muslim Holy Land*, records events that took place when the black rock was stolen from its place in the Kaaba by the "heretical sect known as the Qarmatians" (123):

"The place of the Black Stone in the Honorable House meanwhile remained empty and people put their hands there and kissed it, seeking blessing from its site... The Black Stone remained in the Qarmatians' possession for more than twenty years, in their attempt to attract people to them and in the hope that the Haji would move to their land." (125)

Figure 14-0-5: The Black Stone in the Kaaba.

The frame for the black rock conspicuously resembles the Yoni of the goddess. It faces the east, in the direction of the rising sun and Venus. It's from this point that the faithful begin circling the Kaaba. The skirt conceals the cube-shaped "house" which contains all the idols from pre-Islamic Arabia. As we know, false gods, or idols, are called abominations in the Bible. The Kaaba cube represents a woman with abominations hidden under her skirt. In Genesis 31:34-35, Rachel is pictured as an unclean woman riding atop a beast that is full of abominations. The idols that she stole from her father are HIDDEN beneath her, making her an image of MYSTERY Babylon:

"Now Rachel had taken the images, and put them in the camel's furniture, and sat upon them. And Laban searched all the tent, but found them not. And she said to her father, Let it not displease my lord that I cannot rise up before thee; for the custom of women is upon me. And he searched, but **found not the images**." (Genesis 31:34-35)

The goddess is the "Mother of the Gods" (Mother of Abominations). The cube is a six-sided "Platonic solid" that represents the earth and the material world. As a symbol of the material world, and the goddess, the cube can take on the symbolism of the WOMB. The idols inside the Kaaba are the gods within the womb of the goddess. The word cube (Greek: kybos) is etymologically linked to the goddesses Kybele and Kubaba, and to the Kaaba which is Arabic for "cube."

The "matrix" is a term that people use to describe the world we live in; matrix means womb. Matrix is derived from the word MATER, which—I remind you—means mother. The outline of a cube can resemble a hexagon. The hexagon is a shape that is probably most identified with the honeycomb. All of these symbols point us to the reality that the world we live in is ruled by a "Queen Bee."

Figure 14-0-6: A "Platonic solid" representing the earth in the Classical element system.

Figure 14-0-7: A honeycomb carving in Ephesus, the "City of the Bee," where the "Great Goddess Diana" was worshiped.

CHAPTER 15: THE QUEEN BEE

From the images of beehives in Freemasonic art, to the "Fountain of the Bees" in Rome (a stone image of bees on the clam shell of Venus), even to Popes wearing a crown that looked like a bee's abdomen with a stinger on the top; all of this BEE symbolism begs the question, "Who is the Queen Bee?"

On the page titled, "Goddess as Queen Bee - Artemis of Ephesus," from *Flowering Moon*, it says, "The Bee and the Goddess have been intertwined through time, and in multiple cultures... The honeycomb is seen in architecture in her city of Ephesus – 'City of the Bee'. Her priestesses were called Melissa – a name that means 'bee'. The bee represents the magic of creation, transformation, divine perfection and healing. Artemis as Queen Bee, is the source of all these."

The Lost Art of Resurrection's author, Freddy Silva, gives more insight on the connection between the goddess and bees, saying, "The Greek historian Porphyry describes how in the temples presided by Artemis, Demeter, or Cybele, **the priestesses**-in-attendance were called Melissae - **the bees** - and that this insect came to be associated with the concept of periodic regeneration by the manner in which the Melissae inherited their title from Greek mythology. Melissa was one of a group of bee nymphs whose duty was to teach civilizing behaviors and bring men out of their state of ignorance." (95)

Figure 15-0-1: A plaque showing what is presumed to be a Bee Goddess in the British Museum.

The Queen Bee is the goddess, and the bees represent her priesthood. Silva goes on to say the following about the Queen Bee:

"[ancient societies believed] that wisdom emanated from an Otherworld presided predominantly by **a female deity**, a Mother-Goddess or Divine Virgin who provided hot spots across the Earth where one is perfectly capable of accessing her directly. This exalted maiden represents the creative source; she is the personification of the primeval force. In the Celtic world, such qualities are bestowed upon the goddess Bridhde/Brigit... her name is the root of bride..." (124-125)

"God" or the Force, is manifested in the material world by the goddess. Since bees are a symbol of her priesthood, that must mean that the beehive symbolizes her temple. Is that why architects make buildings with dome-shaped roofs? That's part of it, no doubt. The dome also represents her womb. **St. Peter's Basilica** has a beehive-shaped dome for the womb of the goddess—the Holy of Holies—where Catholic faithful partake of the sacrifice of her son (the eucharist).

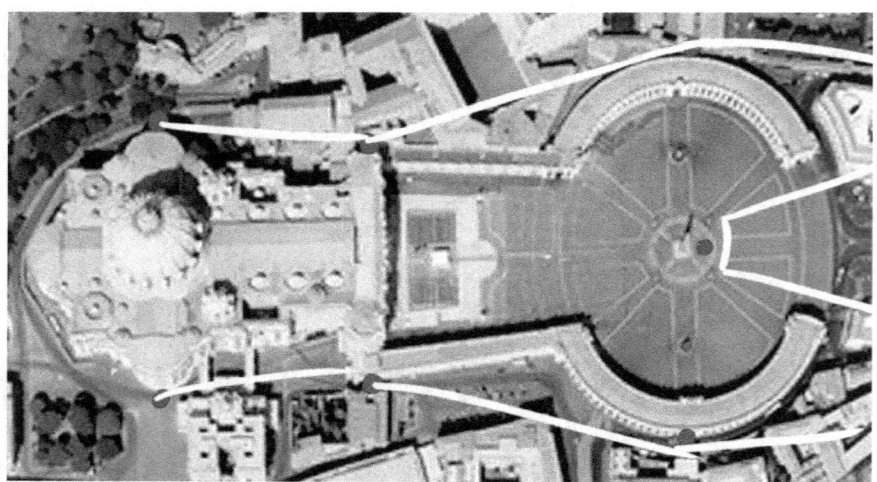

Figure 15-0-2: An aerial view of St. Peter's Basilica square with lines drawn by me to emphasize that it represents a woman's body.

Their children are baptized with the waters of the womb, by priests using a seashell to pour the water. Then the people exit the building and pass through the birth canal, leading to the "key hole," where the phallus of the sun god (the obelisk) penetrates the earth. This obelisk is in St. Peter's **Square**. Remember that the square is a symbol for the Divine Feminine, representing the female reproductive system (YONI). This process of passing through a model of the female reproductive system is how they are purified and "born again."

Freemasonic art shows a beehive with the words "Holiness to the Lord" on it. You will find that beehive on the doorknob of the Salt Lake Mormon Temple as well; and in case you have any doubt that they served the goddess, you can find Venus's seashell on it too.

Figure 15-0-3: Masonic images of beehives with the words "Holiness to the Lord."

You can also find seashells above doors and shelves in the oval office. The oval itself is symbolic of the ovum, which means EGG. The symbols of the Divine Feminine typically all represent either the womb or the vagina. The name VESICA PISCIS is also used. Barbara G. Walker, in *The Women's Encyclopedia of Myths and Secrets* reveals that the word CUNT, which has become vulgar and forbidden to say, comes from the name of a goddess who was the embodiment of the yoni: "[Cunt:] Derivative of the Oriental Great Goddess as Cunti, or Kunda, the Yoni of the Uni-verse." (197)

In the goddess Kunda we have the root for Kundalini, also known as Shakti. As Walker describes Kundalini: "Tantric image of the female serpent coiled in the lowest chakra of the human body, in the pelvis. An aim of Tantric Yoga was to 'realize Kundalini' by certain exercises and meditations, such as yoni-mudra..." (517)

In *America Nation of the goddess*, Alan Butler tells us what YONI symbols are typically most significant: "There is no more potent symbolism for either the Goddess or the sacred feminine generally than the **diamond** and the **Vesica Piscis**." (287)

DIAMOND

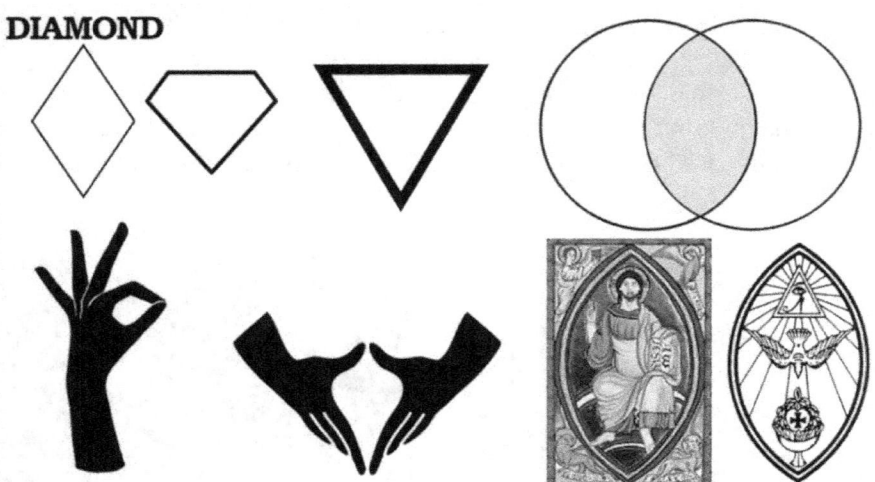

Figure 15-0-4: Symbols representing the Divine Feminine.

The diamond, the downward-pointed triangle, the Vesica Piscis, the Yoni mudra (hand signs), and mandorla; all of these represent the Divine Feminine. Not pictured above but also included are the square and the grail (chalice). What's that Vesica Piscis doing on the Master Card, by the way? That tells you who their master is, that's what. Even the so-called "666 hand-sign" is a YONI mudra.

According to *The Sign Language of the Mysteries*, by J.S.M. Ward, meeting the fingers with the thumb, which creates a ring, is a sign of the Vesica Piscis. It can be combined with other signs such as the "Sign of the Horns." (159-160). Recall all the times you've seen the "okay" hand sign placed over some celebrity's eye; combining the eye and the womb symbolism together—bonus points if you saw them stick out their tongue too.

As to what the yoni hand sign is used to signal, Ward says, "...the initiate is informed that he is a brother of every other member of the Hung lodge because by the ceremony he has been reborn from the same womb, and they speak of their lodge as their 'Mother,' just as a European might speak of his 'Mother City.'" (161) The Mysteries and the lodges where initiates take part in the Mysteries are metaphorical wombs. James G. Frazer, author of *The Golden Bough*, describes the process involving a giant symbol of the YONI by which two particular men had to be "born again":

> "Two Hindoo ambassadors who had been sent to England by a native prince and had returned to India, were considered to have so polluted themselves by contact with strangers that nothing but being born again

could restore them to purity. 'For the purpose of regeneration it is directed to make an image of pure gold of **the female power of nature**, in the shape either of a woman or of a cow.

In this statue the person to be regenerated is enclosed and dragged through the usual channel. As a statue of pure gold and of proper dimensions would be too expensive, it is sufficient to <u>make an image of the sacred Yoni, through which the person to be regenerated is to pass</u>.' Such an image of pure gold was made at the prince's command and his ambassadors were born again by being dragged through it." (157-158)

In relation to being "born again," the spiral represents rebirth. You can find it on the belly of images of goddesses (over their wombs, specifically). The labyrinth, similarly, represents the place where rebirth happens. Emerging from the labyrinth, like rising from the grave, is being reborn—rising as a higher, superior being. It's the "hero's journey." The spiral appears in the title of the movie *Home;* a movie about the search for **a missing mother named Lucy**. It appears in the title of the film *Moana*; a film about a young ocean goddess on a journey to find the missing supreme goddess Tahiti (and find herself while she's at it).

Figure 15-0-5: The "spiral goddesses" bear the spiral on their bellies.

Looking at some of her other symbols, the apple is worthy of discussion. Let's call to mind the Applebee's logo; there are two symbols combined in that name. But what does the apple have to do with the goddess? In one way, it's because the apple is connected to the serpent since it's popularly looked at as the forbidden fruit that the serpent tempted Eve to eat. But how did the apple become synonymous with the knowledge of good and evil? The Bible doesn't say what the forbidden fruit was. It definitely doesn't say that there is anything wrong with eating apples.

Believe it or not, the answer to that also points to the goddess Venus, or Aphrodite, who often holds a golden apple in her hand because it was a prize given to her for winning a beauty contest. The apple is also found in a myth about the golden apples of the garden of the Hesperide nymphs. Their name comes from Hesperus which is a name given to Venus as the evening star. So, it seems, all roads lead to Venus.

Figure 15-0-6: Venus of Arles by François Girardon (1651).

The Holy Grail is a reference to the womb. The chalice and the cup, like the bowl, represents that which contains the holy blood or seed; think about the Rose Bowl. The square, both the four-sided shape and the square tool, are references to the womb as well. The square tool resembles a **V-shape**. The V-shape is also called a chevron. It is symbolic of the chalice which represents the womb.

Figure 15-0-7: The Masonic apron is a square and has square angles. The "V" in the Victoria's Secret logo is a square. The "S" might be for "serpent". Victoria is a goddess and she is also called Nike.

The letter V itself is also a symbol of the Divine Feminine. "V" is the Roman numeral for FIVE. The pentagram has five points. Because of the letter's shape, V also represents the chalice, or grail. Having said that, the **Sigil of Lucifer is shaped like a downward-pointed triangle** (or a chalice). The whole sigil is a YONI symbol. As Dion Fortune explains in *The Mystical Qabalah*: "Cups are essentially the female force, for the cup or chalice is one of the symbols of Binah and is intimately allied with the yoni in esoteric symbolism." (147)

Figure 15-0-8: The Sigil of Lucifer is filled with Divine Feminine symbolism and overall represents the womb. It has an X for the female chromosome, and it also resembles a ROSE.

The **ROSE** is sacred to Venus as a symbol of love and passion, and because the star-point cycle of Venus over the course of eight years makes a rose pattern. I've seen this pattern referred to as the "**Kiss of Venus**." Just like in the past with Venus, in these modern times, roses are given to the Virgin Mary, or Our Lady.

Figure 15-0-9: The "Kiss of Venus" (left) and a rose (right).

As mentioned already, the five-pointed star, often seen in Masonic structures and art, is referred to by the Masons as the "Blazing Star". It is linked to both Venus and Sirius. Not only does Venus make a rose patten over the course of an eight-year cycle but it makes a 5-pointed star as well. The goddess Sopdet, who is identified with Isis, wears a five-pointed star on her head. She is the embodiment of the star Sirius. In *Hidden Secrets of the Eastern Star*, Dr. Cathy Burns comments, "It's interesting to note that Venus also 'became the goddess of the Dog Star, Sirius..." (54)

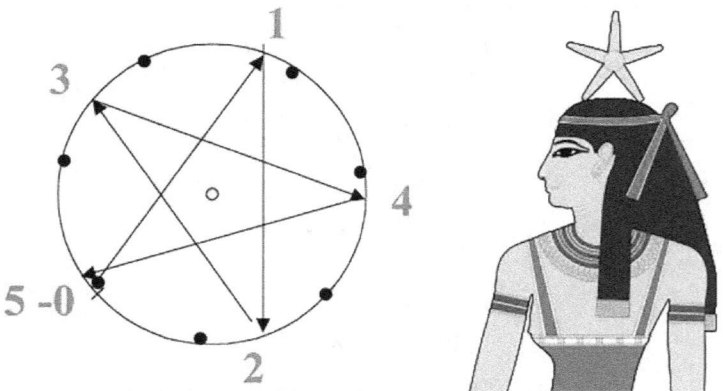

Figure 15-0-10: Pentagram of Venus. (left) Sopdet (Sirius) with the 5-pointed star on her head. (right).

If you have ever wondered why so many countries in the west use the colors red, white, and blue in their flags, it's possibly because Sirius primarily flashes the colors red, white, and blue. Sirius is also called the "Rainbow Star" because a whole spectrum of colors can be observed from the star through a telescope. And if you've ever seen the star through a telescope (you can search for such videos on YouTube, as I have), you will notice that there appears to be a hole in Sirius. The star looks very much like the iris of an EYE. The "Rainbow Star" (Sirius) having the appearance of an eye is interesting because the goddess of the rainbow happens to be named **Iris**. And Iris spelled backwards is Siri (Apple iPhone users would recognize that name).

Considering these many symbols that I've discussed here; how many do we see all around us and how often? It happens much more than you realize; you might start to recognize them from now on. The goddess appears on many types of currency around the world but, since I live in America, I'm going to use this country's money as an example. I've found several examples of United States coins that have goddesses featured on them, either holding the torch of enlightenment or the sprig of regeneration, or even both.

As seen often on the silver dollar is the name of the goddess (Liberty) or the goddess herself. While those coins may say, "In God we trust", you can't allow those flattering words to deceive you. A tree is known by its fruits so look at what they show you. They show you who their "God" (goddess) truly is.

Figure 15-0-11: Various coins featuring the goddess Liberty (Libertas). "In God we trust" is printed on some of them.

"The Mother of Exiles," also known as the Statue of Liberty, stands on Liberty Island in New York Harbor. It's quite clearly the goddess Libertas. By her title, Mother of Exiles, she is the mother of those who have been cast out of their first estate, this perhaps being a reference to fallen angels. The official name for this idol is "**The Statue of Liberty Enlightening the World**." It is made of copper, which is a metal associated with the planet Venus. Held like a child in her left arm is a tablet with the date of the Declaration of Independence on it. America and all its inhabitants are her children.

Stewart Best, in his film "Why America Is Babylon," decoded the Roman numerals MDCCLXXVI (which are also on the tablet); not only does it mean 1776 but it also means 666 after it is decoded. The tablet in the goddess's left arm can also be interpreted as the Beast (the antichrist). It's the mother goddess and her sun again. In Libertas's right arm, is held up the torch. She is the light-bearer, and from her head shines forth the rays of enlightenment.

While the Statue of Liberty may be the most famous symbol of America, she's not called the "spirit of America" or the "goddess of America"; those titles are given to **Columbia**. Columbia comes from columba, meaning a dove. The dove is another one of her symbols. Now people use it as a symbol for the holy spirit, but the Most High didn't tell anyone to do that. He said not to make any image in any likeness of him.

Figure 15-0-12: A roman coin with Venus on the front and her dove on the back.

Figure 15-0-13: Statue of Liberty Enlightening the World.

Figure 15-0-14: The "Goddess of Freedom" which stands on top of the Capitol Building in the District of Columbia.

The capital of the United States is the **District of Columbia** (formerly the Territory of Columbia). The reverence for the Divine Feminine goes beyond just the name here; the entire district is shaped like a diamond (or square). The Potomac River flows through this giant symbol of the yoni. The District of Columbia is surrounded by Maryland on one side, and Virginia on the other. Being on the east coast, this represents the place where the sun is born.

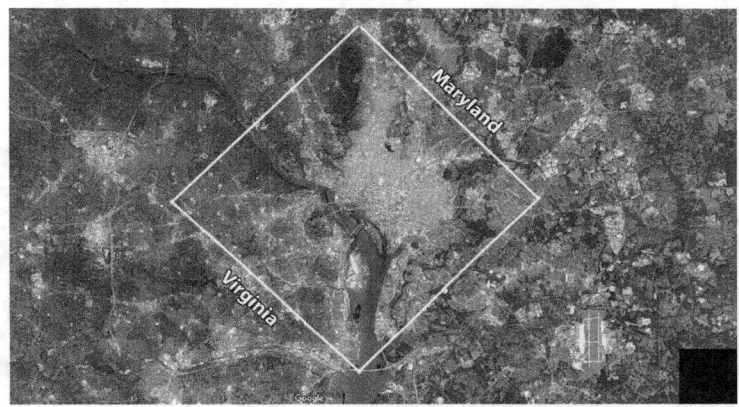

Figure 15-0-15: The District of Columbia.

Inside the District of Columbia is the Pentagon building, which is related to the pentagram, of course. North of the Pentagon is the Whitehouse, where the Oval Office is. It's important that we know the office is oval-shaped because it represents the egg, meaning the seat of power is in the goddess's womb. The White House is located at the southern point of the inverted pentagram that's formed by the street layout.

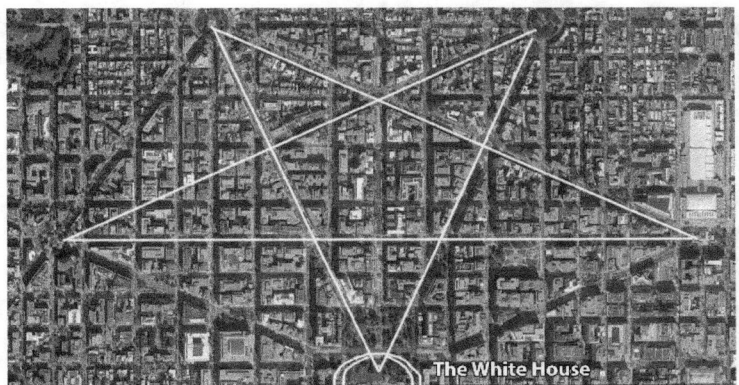

Figure 15-0-16: The White House is located at the tip of a pentagram in the street layout.

To the east, also formed by the street planning, we see a pyramid. Capitol Hill is located just above the capstone of the pyramid. There's an oval in there representing the eye of the capstone. Remember who that EYE on the pedestal (the pyramid) represents—it's that woman called Wickedness. Perched on that capstone is her owl, and inside the owl is the Capitol Building.

You will find the woman who is represented by both the eye symbol and the owl standing on top of the Capitol Building. She's called the "Goddess of Freedom." The word "free" links back to the old Norse goddess Freya; and "liberty" to the goddess Libertas. Ironically, as 2 Peter 2:19 says, "While they promise them liberty, they themselves are the servants of corruption."

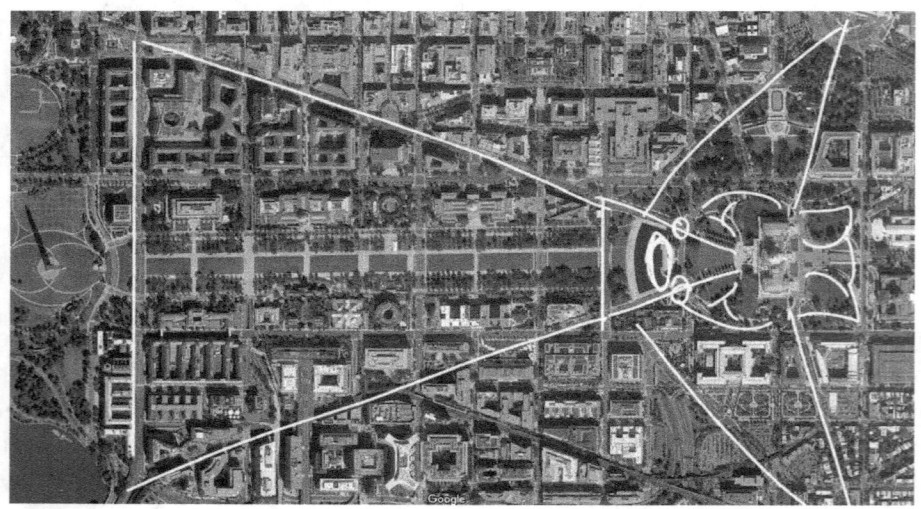

Figure 15-0-17: The Capitol Building is inside the goddess's owl at the top of a pyramid.

Keeping in mind all the Divine Feminine symbolism designed into Washington D.C., I will now inform you that this location is the center of a giant Sigil of Lucifer that spans across nearly a third of the country. "The Seal of Liberty author" has shown how multiple locations across America, all named Cedar Point, were aligned so that when lines are drawn between them, they form the Sigil of Lucifer. In the video titled *Sigil of Lucifer - Scottish Rite's symbol of liberty*, The Seal of Liberty author demonstrates that this could only have been possible with dedicated planning, ruling out any chances of it all being a coincidence.

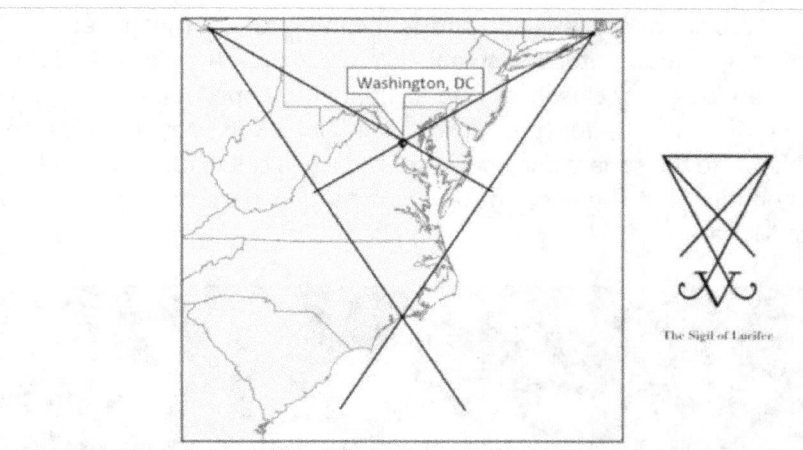

Figure 15-0-18: A screenshot from the video "Sigil of Lucifer - Scottish Rite's symbol of liberty."

The architects of this country didn't do anything without taking extreme care to align their actions with the stars of heaven. Another example of that: on Wednesday, September 18, 1793, the cornerstone was laid for the Capitol Building. Wednesdays are the day of the week most associated with the sign of Virgo. Alan Butler, author of *City of the Goddess*, gives more insight on what was happening in the sky that day:

"If the Goddess of Freedom had already been present on that Wednesday [September 18, 1793], at 3:30am... the near-full moon was about to set, leaving Venus in the east for two hours as the brightest and most significant object in that early autumn morning sky... and the Sun firmly positioned in the sign of Virgo." (13)

There is another striking symbol called the **Auspice Maria**; it is a letter **M** overlaying a letter **A**. In some cases, it's highly stylized, making it difficult to distinguish the letters.

Figure 15-0-19: I overlayed the letter M with the letter A to make the Auspice Maria.

"Auspice Maria" is a Latin phrase meaning "under the protection of Mary." It's another goddess protection symbol like the Sign of the Horns and the Hamsa Hand. If you look very closely at it to examine its shape, you can see a diamond shape in the middle, for the Divine Feminine. You may be able to see a resemblance to the square and compass. And if you call to mind the sigil of Lucifer, you may notice that the very bottom of the sigil, where the V is, resembles the Auspice Maria.

Figure 15-0-20: This banner bears the "Auspice Maria," a symbol that looks similar to the shape at the bottom of the Sigil of Lucifer.

The roman numerals for 911 (IXXI) form the shape of the Auspice Maria. That is surely by design because on September 11 the sun is in the constellation of Virgo (also known as the Celestial Virgin and the Queen of Heaven). In the Roman numerals IXXI, we can also see a representation of 101. The female double-X chromosomes (or double-crosses) form the Sacred Feminine diamond shape. In the Dos Equis logo, there appears to be a sun god in the diamond, perhaps being born from within it.

120

Figure 15-0-21: The female double Xs found in the Auspice Maria and in logos resemble the shape of the square and compass.

Turning our attention to the goddess's owl again: we'll find it in many other places, such as logos and as the symbol of the Illuminati. It stands as a giant stone image at Bohemian Grove, where influential men go to perform rituals and worship "Great Nature," which we know is the Great Whore of Babylon. Out there, in the grove, they reject the Most High Yah, referring to Him as "Dull Care," in a ceremony called the "Cremation of Care." The goddess was also found on the Georgia Guidestones, under the name "Nature," before the Guidestones were unceremoniously toppled in 2022.

Figure 15-0-22: The Bohemian Club logo.

The first commandment on the Georgia Guidestones was, "Maintain humanity under 500,000,000 in perpetual balance with [N]ature." The tenth and the final commandment was, "Be not a cancer on the Earth — Leave room for [N]ature — Leave room for [N]ature." **Nature** was mentioned three times. In the final commandment, the commandment to leave room for Nature was written twice.

When Masons say "nature," I know they mean it with a capital N, because it is a spirit. That much is made clear when you hear them praise "**Great Nature**" in video footage from Bohemian Grove. They might as well call her Asherah. In modern times, we call Asherah by the names Mother Earth, Mother Nature, or Gaia. Gaia is a name that is at the center of the New Age movement.

Dr. John Rodgers, who wrote the *New Age Bible*, said, "The New Age movement seemed to come into being during the 60s and 70s, but actually it is much older than that. The roots of the New Age movement can be traced to as early as 1776, when a new and revolutionary form of government was created in America. The founders of this nation designed a 'Great Seal' to be the symbol of this new form of government, and on the Great Seal are found the words: 'NOVUS ORDO SECULARUM,' which means '**A new order of the ages**.'" (96)

MYSTERY Babylon is hidden in far more symbols than I could possibly hope to show you in one book. I will give a few more examples. In a screenshot from the video for the song "Mother," Mehgan Trainor wears silver (the color of the moon) and sits in the sacred feminine diamonds/squares. Light rays expand outward. These symbols vaguely resemble the shape of an eye, as well.

Figure 15-0-21: The diva in Divine Feminine symbolism in the music video "Mother" (2023).

While goddess symbols are often hidden in plain sight (as with Mastercard's Vesica Piscis), sometimes they are inverted into masculine forms, for purpose of obfuscation. The symbol for Lucis Trust, formerly known as Lucifer

Publishing Company, is a triangle with the word LUX (light) designed into it. This is an inverted Sigil of Lucifer.

L U C I S   **Sigil of Lucifer**

Figure 15-0-22: The Mastercard logo (left) is a Vesica Piscis. The Lucis Trust logo (right) is an inverted sigil of Lucifer.

I don't doubt that Lucifer will receive worship as a male, as I pointed out when discussing "Allah," but her true nature as a female will eventually show itself. This is typically done in ways the uninitiated can't perceive (in religious rituals, entertainment, logos, and Masonic art). "MYSTERY Babylon" is a **MYSTERY**, so the initiated must present Lucifer as a male to the outsider, and Lucis Trust (Lucifer Publishing Company) does exactly that.

Figure 0-23: The Columbia Pictures logo.

Ishtar was the "Goddess of Light" in Babylon, and we still see the goddess bringing the light from heaven in other forms. A most notable example is in the Columbia Pictures logo, which features the goddess Columbia holding the torch of enlightenment. The model who posed for the 1992 logo held in her hand an electric lamp that resembled a torch. When we see the image of a woman holding up a light, it's not merely a creative choice being made; it's Ishtar, the goddess of light (Lucifer), being shown to us under a different persona.

123

Das elektrische Licht. Gemälde von Ludwig Kandler.

Nach einer Photographie von Dr. E. Albert in München.

Figure 15-0-23: "The Electric Light" by Ludwig Kandler (1884).

CHAPTER 16: I AM, AND NONE ELSE BESIDE ME

Isis is the most important figure in Freemasonry. Just as with Kali, there are direct references to her in Bible prophecy. Isaiah chapter 47 is such a prophecy. In this chapter, she is called "the virgin daughter of Babylon," "the widow," and "the lady of kingdoms". You'll see that God is not just addressing a city in this chapter, but the SPIRIT of Babylon that rules over this city. Starting at verse 1:

"Come down, and sit in the dust, O virgin daughter of Babylon, **sit on the ground: there is no throne**, O daughter of the Chaldeans: for thou shalt no more be called tender and delicate." (Isaiah 47:1)

This first verse is a direct shot at Isis's name. When the Most High tells her, "Sit on the ground: there is no throne," that jumps off the page to me. Why would He say such a thing unless the subject of the prophecy had some kind of connection to a throne? **Isis's name means THRONE.** She is the personification of the throne in Egypt and wears an image of a throne on her head. One must be her offspring (or SEED) to even sit on her lap, which is the symbol of the throne. Verse 2 says:

"Take the millstones, and grind meal: uncover thy locks, make bare the leg, uncover the thigh, pass over the rivers. **Thy nakedness shall be uncovered**, yea, thy shame shall be seen: I will take vengeance, and I will not meet thee as a man." (Isaiah 47:2-3)

Here the Most High Yah is saying that he is going to unveil her; he's going to discover all of her secrets places. Passing over the rivers, or the private areas, and exposing her nakedness. He's giving the image of snatching the covering off a harlot to reveal her shame. Have you ever heard of the Veil of Isis? The Veil represents Isis's secrets—**her Mysteries**. From *Isiopolis*, on the veil of Isis:

"There are a few other ancient references to the veil of Isis. The Greco-Egyptian magical papyri refer to it on several occasions. In one, the magician invokes Isis and asks Her to remove Her veil in order to reveal the future and 'shake destiny.' By revealing the Mysteries beneath Her veil, the magician hoped that the Goddess Who was worshiped as Lady of Fate and Fortune could not only predict, but could change or 'shake' destiny... **The unveiling of the Goddess became a symbol of the**

revelation of esoteric secrets, sometimes specifically the revelation of Egyptian secrets."

At the Herbert Hoover National Historic Site, there is a statue of Isis that is veiled and bears a significant inscription from her temple in Sais. I will explain what that inscription is and what it means later in this chapter, because it is directly referenced by the book of Isaiah in chapter 47.

Figure 16-0-1: Statue of Isis by Auguste Puttemans at the Herbert Hoover National Historic Site.

The first three verses of this chapter are too specific to be dismissed as a coincidence. We'll see even more references to Isis as we read on.

"As for our redeemer, the LORD of hosts is his name, the Holy One of Israel. Sit thou silent, and get thee into darkness, <u>O daughter of the Chaldeans</u>: for thou shalt no more be called, **The lady of kingdoms**." (Isaiah 47:4-5)

The Queen of Heaven had the most important cults in Babylon and Ur, the land of the Chaldees. The modern version of the Queen of Heaven, the Virgin Mary, is **called the Lady of All Nations**. Another word for nations is KINGDOMS. This is another reference to the goddess, confirming that this prophecy against the "virgin daughter of Babylon" also has a spiritual subject. Verse 6 says:

"I was wroth with my people, I have polluted mine inheritance, and given them into thine hand: thou didst shew them no mercy; upon the ancient hast thou very heavily laid thy yoke. And thou saidst, I shall be a lady for ever: so that thou didst not lay these things to thy heart, neither didst remember the latter end of it." (Isaiah 47:6-7)

The Most High God, Yah, sent Israel into captivity in Babylon, and this goddess which ruled over Babylon laid VERY heavy the yoke of iron around their necks. Verse 8 reads:

"Therefore hear now this, thou that art given to pleasures, that dwellest carelessly, that sayest <u>in thine heart</u>, I am, and none else beside me; **I shall not sit as a widow**, neither shall I know the loss of children:" (Isaiah 47:8)

In Freemasonry, Isis is called "the Widow". The Masons are called "Widow's sons" or "Sons of the Widow". Every Freemason, every president, and every king is pictured as the child sitting on Isis's lap. **They are the seed of the serpent**, and the serpent proclaims here that she shall not know the loss of her children. Eve has her righteous children, and Babylon has her unrighteous children. She also says in her heart, "I AM, AND NONE ELSE BESIDE ME." This is a declaration by her that SHE is GOD.

In Isaiah 45:5, the Most High God Yahawah says, "**I am** the LORD, and **there is none else**, there is no God beside me." When the virgin daughter of Babylon says in her heart, "**I am, and none else beside me**," (Isaiah 47:8) that is a declaration of rebellion against the Most High, in the same spirit as Lucifer saying in Isaiah 14:14, "I will be like the Most High." She goes on to say in Isaiah 47:8 that she shall not sit (or remain) as a widow. This is yet another reference to Isis who is called **the Widow**.

"But these two things shall come to thee in a moment in one day, the loss of children, and widowhood: they shall come upon thee in their perfection for the multitude of **thy sorceries**, and for the great abundance of thine enchantments." (Isaiah 47:9)

God tells Isis that she will be a widow and that she will know the loss of children, and this will be for the multitude of her SORCERIES. This draws a connection to Isaiah 57:3-4, where the goddess Kali is directly referenced. It reads:

"But draw near hither, ye sons of **the sorceress**, the seed of the adulterer and the whore. Against whom do ye sport yourselves? against whom **make ye a wide mouth, and draw out the tongue**? are ye not children of transgression, a seed of falsehood," (Isaiah 57:3-4)

God calls her THE SORCERESS, and he mentions the act of making a wide mouth and drawing out the tongue (like Kali), an act which is directed against Him. He calls the fornicators involved in her worship the "children of transgression" (or children of WICKEDNESS). Verse 10 in Isaiah 47 says:

"For thou hast trusted in thy wickedness: thou hast said, **None seeth me**. Thy wisdom and thy knowledge, it hath perverted thee; and thou hast said in thine heart, **I am, and none else beside me**." (Isaiah 47:10)

As the MYSTERY of Iniquity, and MYSTERY Babylon, Isis thinks that NONE SEE HER. However, God has already promised to remove her veil and expose her nakedness. And then she says a second time... IN HER HEART, "I am, and none else beside me." It is said twice so that we can't miss it. The Most High God wouldn't bother to include these words from the Great Whore in His prophetic scriptures TWICE if it wasn't extremely important.

In the temple of Isis at Sais are inscribed the words, "**I - Isis - am all that has been, that is, or shall be; No mortal man hath ever me unveiled**." Is that not exactly what we've been reading in Isaiah 47? She says in her heart, "None seeth me" and "I am, and none else beside me." This is no coincidence. The "virgin daughter of Babylon" is a spirit who is being directly confronted in Isaiah chapter 47.

In *The Lost Keys of Freemasonry*, Manly P. Hall says of Freemasonry and its connection to Isis:

"Enter the temple in reverence, for it is in truth the dwelling place of a <u>Great Spirit</u>, **the Spirit of Masonry**. Masonry is an ordainer of kings." (90)

We will fully expose that "Great Spirit" of Freemasonry before we're done here. Manly P. Hall gives a name for the "Spirit of Freemasonry":

"**Freemasonry as an institution is Isis**, the mother of Mysteries, from whose dark womb the Initiates are born in the mystery of the second or philosophic birth. Thus all adepts, by virtue of their participation in the rites, are figuratively, at least, the Sons of Isis. As Isis is the Widow, seeking to restore her lord, and to avenge his cruel murder, it follows that all Master Masons or Master Builders, are widow's sons." (153)

Isis is called the Widow because her husband Osiris was murdered by the often-antagonistic god Set. My own discernment, by the grace of the Most High, brought me to the understanding that the Egyptian god Set is also associated with the Hebrew God, Yahawah (YHWH). I believe the name Set, came from Adam's son Seth. Noah and Shem kept the truth of the Most High God through the flood. Then, Yahawah became identified with the Egyptian god Set because of events surrounding the Tower of Babel. This is where the tower of Babel itself becomes the source of the myth of the death of Osiris. As we read in Genesis 11:8-9:

"**So the LORD scattered them abroad from thence upon the face of all the earth**: and they left off to build the city. Therefore is the name of it called Babel; because the LORD did there confound the language of all the earth: and from thence did the LORD scatter them abroad upon the face of all the earth." (Genesis 11:8-9)

Yah stopped the tower from being built and scattered the builders across the earth. That story is reflected in the Egyptian myth where Set murdered the sun god Osiris and scattered his body parts across the earth. As was revealed earlier in this chapter, the Bible refers to Isis as "the virgin daughter of Babylon." Therefore, Babylon represents Isis, and the builders are her husbands (and also her children). Now that her metaphorical husband has been slain, Isis becomes a widow—the Black Widow—and it's her goal to regather the pieces of her husband's body and resurrect him as her child, Horus.

In the Egyptian myth, Isis is able to find all the pieces except for the phallus of Osiris. The phallus is the generative principle in the male. It also symbolizes "the lost Word" in Freemasonry. Typically, the obelisk, which can also serve as a sundial, represents the phallus of the slain sun god. The goddess creates a substitute which she uses to conceive, and she rebirths her husband in the form of her son (who is "the Word"). The broken pillar (or obelisk) represents the slain sun god and the unfinished tower of Babel. It's Isis's mission to avenge the murder of her husband against Set. Horus, Isis's son, is the one who exacts this revenge in mythology. This can be symbolic of Babylon's son, the Beast from the bottomless pit, defeating the true God (Yahawah) who is the adversary in the eyes of the Egyptians.

When the Luciferians speak of "Satan," Yaldaboath, or Saklas, they are referring to the true God (YHWH). He is also called the Demiurge, as mentioned earlier. Yahawah has commandments and requires His children to come out from among evil doers and be separate. Because He stands against their forms of "enlightenment," they claim that the Hebrew God is blind and ignorant.

In Freemasonry, the direction of the North (where God's throne is) is regarded as a place of darkness where there is no light. On the Masonic tracing boards, you may notice that the directions of the North, East, South, and West are not arranged like they are on a compass. The East is where the North would be on a compass. The East is where the sun, moon, and Blazing Star are. The All-Seeing Eye is sometimes where Venus/Sirius, represented by the Blazing Star would be. The North is on the left side of the board, where the West would be on a compass. Not only is the Most High's throne in the "sides of the north," but—as the word tells us in Malachi 3:6—Yah says, "For I am the LORD, I change not." James 1:17 says of Him, "...with whom is no variableness, neither shadow of turning." The North star (Polaris) is a star that doesn't change and shows no degree of movement. There's no doubt in my mind that the North Star represents the Most High. It's both the most-North and the most-high star. It represents the unmovable Truth that we can use to navigate the world we live in, contrary to the strange woman (Lucifer) whose ways are moveable so that we can't know them.

Figure 16-0-2: "Alma Mater" statue by Daniel Chester French (1903) at Columbia University.

Figure 16-0-3: First Degree Tracing Board by Josiah Bowring (1819), showing the Genius of Freemasonry as a triple goddess.

CHAPTER 17: WISE AS SERPENTS, HARMLESS AS DOVES

The two pillars on either side of the door of the temple represent two opposites. These pillars are represented by various symbols all around us. Jesus Christ is the door to the kingdom of heaven and to eternal life; he stands between two olive trees. He said himself in John 3:19, "**I am the door**: by me if any man enter in, he shall be saved, and shall go in and out, and find pasture." When Samson was placed between the two pillars, he brought the two opposites (the roof and the floor) together, and by his sacrifice he destroyed his enemies, above and below.

In the same way, when Jesus Christ was crucified between two thieves, he brought the kingdom of darkness down. As he said in John 12:32, "...if I be lifted up from the earth, will draw all men unto me." And in John 12:31, he said, "Now is the judgment of this world: now shall the prince of this world be cast out."

Unlike with Lucifer, however, there is no duality with Jesus Christ. 1 John 1:5 says, "This then is the message which we have heard of him, and declare unto you, that God is light, and in him is NO darkness at all." Lucifer identifies herself as "the Whore" AND "the Holy One." The goddess is full of duality. She is the Morning and the Evening star, light and darkness. As the diva, Meredith Brooks, sang in her song titled "Bitch": "I'm a child, I'm a mother, I'm a sinner, I'm a saint, I do not feel ashamed."

As both the dove and the serpent are animals sacred to the goddess, she is both a devil and an angel of light. Knowledge of good and evil. This is the Masonic checkerboard floor; opposites must be embraced as being part of one whole. I learned of the place that the goddess held between the two pillars simply by observing the symbols that I was constantly being shown in artwork and in music videos. In *The Secret Teachings of all Ages,* Manly P. Hall confirms what I was able to discover (by the grace of the Most High):

"The World Virgin is sometimes shown standing between two great pillars—the Jachin and Boaz of Freemasonry—symbolizing the fact that Nature attains productivity by means of polarity. **As wisdom personified, Isis stands between the pillars of opposites**, demonstrating that understanding is always found at the point of equilibrium and that truth is often crucified between the two thieves of apparent contradiction." (130)

The two pillars are bridged by the goddess. The above and the below. The spirit and the material. Lucifer is the Mystery religion's "Jacob's ladder," bridging the gap between heaven and earth. For those who believe in a trinity, Mary has become the third person in that trinity, becoming like the Most High (in accordance with Lucifer's "I WILL" statements in Isaiah 14).

Figure 17-0-1: "The Coronation of the Virgin" by Diego Velázquez (1635–1636).

In much of the art she's in, there is a direct line between Mary and the dove: they are one and the same (remember that the dove is a goddess symbol). Those pillars on either side of Mary can be angels, candle sticks, or even two men who are supposed to represent "God the Son" and "God the Father". Each pillar represents the number one. The zero is the doorway, the YONI. The number 101 is typically used to signify something that is basic or introductory. It's the point of initiation.

Caitlin Matthews, author of *Sophia: Goddess of Wisdom, Bride of God*, comments on the goddess identifying as a "holy" whore:

"Sophia also appears in the surprising guise of a harlot. This theme is traceable from the Sumerian Epic of Gilgamesh, in which the divine barmaid of the gods, Siduri, consoles Gilgamesh and a mortal hierodule initiates Enkidu into manhood, right through to the medieval conflation of the Magdalene with the woman taken in adultery. This image of the harlot is perfectly reasonable in the context of gnosis, for she is a woman of initiatory knowledge. **'It is I who am the harlot: and the holy'** says the Thunder-Perfect voice of Sophia. The images of the whore and the holy one are blended in gnosis as they are throughout biblical tradition." (162)

In their book, *Jesus and the Lost Goddess*, Timothy Freke and Peter Gandy touch on how the duality of Sophia manifests:

"In the gospels the Virgin Mary and Mary Magdalene represent the higher Sophia and the fallen Sophia. They are called by the same name to emphasize the fact that mythologically **they are aspects of the same figure**. As in the Sophia myth, the first Mary is a virgin, like Sophia when she was living with her Father, and the second is a prostitute who is redeemed by her lover Jesus, like Sophia when lost in the world." (95)

Figure 17-0-2: "God is Wild (Film)" by Tommy Genesis. MMXVIII Downtown Records.

The point is illustrated in the short film *God is Wild* by Tommy Genesis, as the diva in the video stands between the two pillars, showing both demonic and angelic traits; she is the bridge between both worlds. On her waist is a key representing WISDOM, which resembles the sign for female (Venus) or for the womb.

Perhaps Sophia even bridges the gap between female and male; this is what we typically think of when the Baphomet is mentioned. One thing that needs to be said when discussing **Baphomet** is the fact that the famous image of the hermaphroditic Baphomet that was drawn by the French occultist, Eliphas

Levi, wasn't drawn until FIVE HUNDRED YEARS after the Templar order had been dissolved. It's very unlikely that Levi's drawing of the Baphomet had anything to do with the Baphomet that the Templars were accused of worshiping.

Figure 17-0-3: Eliphas Levi's drawing of Baphomet (1861).

The inspiration for the famous drawing of the goat-headed figure is most assuredly the Bible. Levi's drawing of Baphomet appears to incorporate everything that Yahawah told the Israelites to avoid making a graven image of, or worshiping, in Deuteronomy chapter 4:

"Take ye therefore good heed unto yourselves; for ye saw no manner of similitude on the day that the LORD spake unto you in Horeb out of the midst of the fire: Lest ye corrupt yourselves, and make you a graven image, the similitude of any figure, the likeness of **male or female**, The likeness of **any beast** that is on the earth, the likeness of any **winged fowl** that flieth in the air, The likeness of **any thing that creepeth** on the ground, the likeness of **any fish** that is in the waters beneath the earth: And lest thou lift up thine eyes unto heaven, and when thou seest **the sun, and the moon, and the stars**, even all the host of heaven, shouldest be driven to worship them, and serve them…" (Deuteronomy 4:15-19)

This drawing might not have anything to do with the original Baphomet at all, which—at the time—was believed to be the head of a bearded man. But as Alan Butler says in *The Goddess, the Grail & the Lodge*:

"This head may also have related John the Baptist, for whom the Templars had a special reverence. Even more likely is the suggestion that the bearded head could have represented the 'Green Man.' Effigies of the Green man are to be seen in many Gothic churches and cathedrals... Few historians now doubt that the Green Man is a hangover from the days of nature worship and, in particular, worship of the Goddess." (222)

The Templars' reverence for John the Baptist is likely due to his similarity to the "Green Man," a god of nature. John dwelled in the wilderness, wearing camel hair and eating locusts and wild honey. John the Baptist was beheaded and the Green Man is typically depicted as a head with no body; it's not hard to see how the Templars made the connection. Alan Butler reveals what the truth about Baphomet is when the name is put through a substitution cipher, as first discovered by the British Bible scholar Dr. Hugh Schonfield:

"In all probability, the name Baphomet had nothing to do with the mysterious bearded head of the Templars, and the confusion may have been due to the ineptitude on the part of Phillip IV's interrogators. However, the word was still of tremendous importance to the Templars because once it has gone through the mill of the Atbash Cipher, Baphomet comes out as '**Sophia**." (222-223)

The image of "Baphomet" drawn by Eliphas Levi was evidently his own creation, using Deuteronomy 4:15-19 as his inspiration. I can't rule out that he did know that **Baphomet was a codeword for Sophia** (Wisdom) somehow, but the revelation of the true meaning of "Baphomet" makes so much more sense because the Templars were famously Marianist, as Alan Butler explains:

"...The Templars were dedicated to the Virgin Mary, for whom they showed what amounted to an obsession. This had also been true of their founder, St. Bernard of Clairvaux. Bernard had deliberately manipulated the Catholic Church of his day to virtually deify Mary. **The Templar Order was accused of worshipping Baphomet, which we know is a code word and which really means Sophia.** Sophia, in turn is early Christian speak for the Holy Spirit, often represented as a dove. The dove has represented the Goddess for thousands of years. It seems more and more likely that the true religious imperatives of the Templars meant that, in fourteenth-century Christian terms, they were 'guilty as charged." (223)

The Queen of Heaven, Baphomet, was the goddess that the Templars worshiped in the forms of the two Marys of duality—Mary the virgin mother of Jesus, and Mary Magdalene, out of whom Jesus Christ cast seven devils. Sophia was the Holy Grail. It wasn't an actual cup; the grail is a reference to the womb.

Figure 17-0-4:" The Damsel of the Sanct Grael" by Dante Gabriel Rossetti (1874).

Like the ankh symbol, the chalice or grail symbolizes the source of life. And being that the tomb is the womb of Mother Earth, these symbols also represent spiritual rebirth (or literal death and resurrection). The Holy Grail in the Catholic ceremonies represents the womb of the Virgin Mary. It's not likely a confession that any priest will make, but as observers we can clearly see with our own eyes that Mary holds a place in the Trinity next to God and His Son. In the very detailed book, *Freemasonry: Rituals, Symbols & History of the Secret Society*, Mark Stavish explains what Mary represents in the minds of the Freemasons, comparing her to "geometry":

> "It is interesting to note that when the building phase occurred, many if not all the great cathedrals, and to a fair extent the smaller ones as well, were dedicated to 'Our Lady,' or the Virgin Mary, the mother of Jesus Christ. Herein we see **the material world giving birth or expression to divine ideals**, taking them from the abstract and making them tangible, concrete, living." (88)

> "It is through Mary that the Word is 'made flesh' and through geometry that ideal becomes form. The Lost Word that each Master Mason seeks... is the power of creation itself. Mary is the Wisdom Seat, the foundation of all creation in the medieval mind, and the Word is her offspring. **The power of creation is found in Wisdom**." (105)

Figure 17-0-5: An image of the Chalice (Holy Grail) inside of a Sacred Feminine diamond.

As Mark said, geometry is personified by a goddess; through geometry, ideas can be given form in the material world. Goddesses personify a lot of concepts in Freemasonry. It underlines the point that the Divine Feminine (Lucifer) is the source of enlightenment. Knowing that Geometry is a spirit in Freemasonry, I believe it's fitting to put a capital "G" on the word to emphasize that and help us to remember it.

In *A Dictionary of Freemasonry*, Robert Macoy explains the connection of the letter "G" to Geometry, and how important it is. He gives us good reasons to believe that the letter G truly does stand for geometry:

"[The letter G] is deservedly regarded as one of the most sacred of the Masonic emblems... This symbol proves that Freemasonry always prosecuted its labors with reference to the grand ideas of Infinity and Eternity [b]y **the letter G**—which conveyed to the minds of the brethren, at the same time, the idea of God and that of Geometry—**it bound heaven to earth**, the divine to the human, and the infinite to the finite." (152)

"[The letter G] cannot allude to the name of God alone in the German lodges, or it could not be found in the situation in foreign lodges. **It has a closer affinity to Geometry**, which is so necessary to an Architect, and geometrical certainty and truth is everywhere necessary." (519)

"Among the mathematical sciences geometry is the one which has the most especial reference to architecture, and we can, therefore, under the name of **geometry**, understand the whole art of Freemasonry. In Anderson's *Book of Constitutions*, **Freemasonry is frequently called geometry**; and of the latter he saith that the whole being of the Order is comprehended in it. Freemasons therefore ought to make themselves intimately acquainted with geometry. It is not absolutely necessary to be able to delineate geometrical figures; but it is necessary to be able to deduce all our actions, works, or resolutions from geometrical principles." (519-520)

As Macoy said, the letter G represents something that bounds heaven to earth. Mark Stavish said that "something" was Geometry. I said that it was the goddess, who also stands between the two pillars of opposites. Stavish expounds on geometry, and also introduces us to the "Genius of Freemasonry":

"We often hear of the **Genius of Freemasonry** referred to as 'she' and discussed in anthropomorphic terms—expressing human qualities, but on a perfected or archetypal level... This symbol, then, takes on a deeper connection to both a literal spiritual force protecting Freemasonry and the Gnostic notions of **the Divine Sophia**, or Wisdom—the Bride of God." (75-76)

Manly P. Hall also said that there was a "Great Spirit" that guided Freemasonry, and he said that Isis was the Mother of the Mysteries. That would make Isis a name for the Genius of Freemasonry too. Mark Stavish called this spirit that protected Freemasonry "the Divine Sophia." He also says of her, "[The Genius of Freemasonry] is **the guiding spirit of Freemasonry** and every Mason who seeks to understand its mysteries..." (89)

Figure 17-0-6: The General Manual of Freemasonry (1883) (left) and Masonic Esotericism 1st third of 19th century (right)..

The Genius of Freemasonry is the Wisdom goddess that goes by many names: Sophia, Athena, Shekinah, Shakti, and Isis (to name some).

Figure 17-0-7: An illustration of "The Blazing Star" with the letter G on it.

Stavish agrees with Macoy, in the following quote, that the Masonic G represents Geometry. "**[The] G stands for geometry**, the most critical field of learning for any educated person, particularly one who would be in the building trades." (84) Now, Mark reveals that geometry too is essentially the goddess of Freemasonry:

"Like **'geometry' and 'wisdom' in the form of Sophia** before it, the tendency to turn abstract forces and ideals into anthropomorphic images, particularly of a feminine form, suggests pre-Christian sources in classical paganism... One woodcut shows **geometry personified as a beautiful woman**, complete with the letter G and surrounded by the working tools of the building trade..." (89)

The G is the woman that we see in Masonic art, often weeping over the broken pillar. Whether she is called Wisdom, Geometry, or the Genius of Freemasonry, it's the same goddess, represented by the Blazing Star (the pentagram). She is MYSTERY, Babylon. While I may not be convinced of what Macoy and Stavish say about the meaning of the G being "Geometry," I don't think they're wrong either. The G is indeed surrounded by the tools that are used to measure the material world. I'm inclined to believe that **the G stands for Gaia**, the personification of the Earth. Gaia is a universally recognized name that encompasses all the names of other goddesses, including the goddess which personifies "Geometry," which means "measurement of earth."

Figure 17-0-8: Masonic Register. Symbolic History of F. and A.M (1876).

As the "world soul" (Anima Mundi), **Gaia** is the expression of the Force in the material world. She is the "face of God" or "presence of God." As the bridge between worlds, **she is the "G"** between the compass and square, in the **sacred feminine diamond**. The "G" is sometimes replaced by a 5-pointed star.

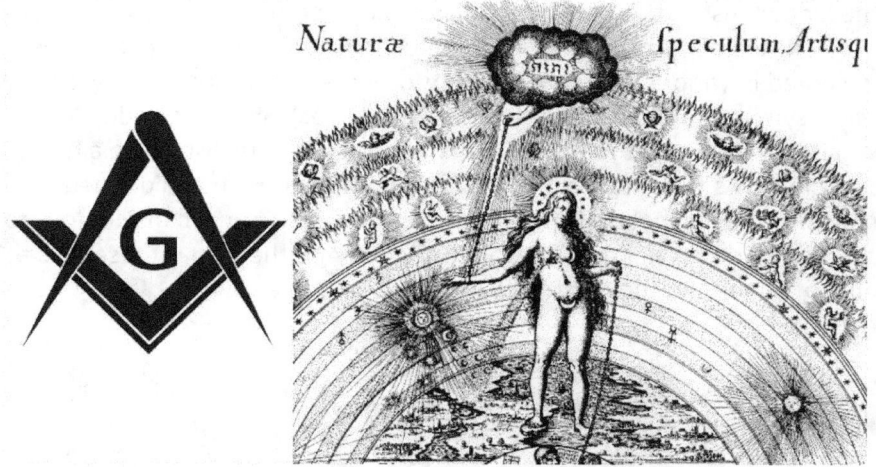

Figure 17-0-9: The Masonic Square and Compass (left) and the Anima Mundi (right).

On Masonic tracing boards, you will notice Jacob's ladder (or a stairway to heaven), and typically the triple goddesses are on that ladder.

Figure 17-0-10: First Degree Tracing Board by Josiah Bowring (1819).

One of the women is the virgin, one of them is the mother, and one is the old woman (Fate/Fortuna). One has a book on her lap where a child would sit; that book represents the word (the word is her seed). Her reading a book could also show that she is Wisdom. The key (a symbol for Wisdom) is tied to the ladder. The virgin is holding an anchor to show that she cannot be moved; she is bound to the ladder, just as the Anima Mundi is chained between heaven and earth.

These goddesses that are venerated in Freemasonry have also been represented in various fairy tales. Beauty, or Belle, in the story *Beauty and the Beast*, is symbolic of Freemasonry (or the Mysteries). She's the goddess of Freemasonry who raises man who is in his lowest, beastly estate, to a higher, evolved form. As the rough-cut stone becomes the smooth and defined cube on the Masonic tracing board, Beauty changes the Beast into a man. Her love for books also identifies her as a Wisdom Goddess. And the rose is present as a symbol of Venus and the Mysteries.

Figure 17-0-11: Beauty from Beaumont's Beauty and the Beast (1756).

As with "Beauty," I've noticed that some other names from fairy tales are codewords for Lucifer, such as "Alice" from *Alice in Wonderland*. The journey down the rabbit hole is used as a metaphor for initiation into the Mysteries. The rabbit from the story is a sacred animal and fertility symbol long associated with Ishtar. Alice, having made her journey into the Mysteries and confronted the passionate scarlet queen in her own heart, emerges as a wisdom goddess.

The wicked witch, or old crone, in stories such as *Snow White* is the goddess of fate called Fortuna. She is winter and death battling the young and fertile queen of the earth. Also called Lady Luck (Lady Lux) and Destiny, she is there at the end of the ladder (the end of life) on the Masonic tracing board. In *Ancient Mirrors of Womanhood*, Merlin Stone sheds some light on other identities of "Lady Luck":

"Celtic memories of the great Queen Morgan also lingered in the Italian lands, where tales were told of Fata Morgana who lived beneath the waters of a lake. But Bojardo wrote that the powerful Fata Morgana was but another name for the holy Goddess Fortuna. She whose shrines once graced Etruscan towns where omens of the future bubbled forth from underground springs. And there are those who say that Fata and Fortuna were but other names for the Three who were known as The Fates..." (61)

As the moon and serpent represent death and rebirth, so does the goddess. Dion Fortune, author of *The Mystical Qabalah* explains the duality assigned to the third sephirot in Kabbalah, called Binah:

"...the Great Mother aspect and the Saturn aspect, for both these attributions are given to Binah. **She is the mighty Mother of All Living, and she is also the death principle**; <u>for the giver of life in form is also the giver of death</u>, for form must die when its use is outworn. Upon the planes for form, death and birth are the two sides of the same coin... The mother aspect of Binah finds expression in the title of Marah, the Sea, which is given to her. It is a curious fact that Venus-Aphrodite is represented as being born from the sea foam, and the Virgin Mary is called by Catholics Stella Maris, Star of the Sea. The word Marah, which is the root of Mary, also means bitter, and the spiritual experience attributed to Binah is the Vision of Sorrow. A vision which calls to mind the picture of the Virgin weeping at the foot of the Cross, her heart pierced by seven swords." (144)

As Dion Fortune said, "She is the mighty Mother of All Living, and she is also the death principle." The tomb is the womb of mother earth. Rebirth is a focal point in the Mysteries because the initiates understand the axiom, as the Bible says in 1 Corinthians 15:36, "That which thou sowest is not quickened, except it die." Indeed, it was by one man's sin—Adam's sin—that death came into the world. But the woman, who was called Eve because she was the "mother of all living," was the giver of death.

Figure 17-0-12: The goddess and the serpent in Eden. (public domain, artist unknown).

CHAPTER 18: BABYLON IS FALLEN, IS FALLEN

In the time of the end, I believe there will be a deconstruction of the three main religions based on the Bible. Judaism, Christianity, and Islam, as institutions, will be manipulated into acting as destructive forces—each convinced of their own righteousness—that will force people to either remain faithful to them or abandon them. It will also be widely believed that these religions were built on lies; and for the most part, they were. Babylon has controlled what the world knows as "Christianity" since Constantine had his supposed conversion experience. All of these major religions are under her control, and once the restrainer is removed (2 Thessalonians 2:7), Lucifer will make her big move to put herself back on top as the supreme deity. It's the goddess who will unite all the religions of the world under three key principles:

1. "God" is one with creation (meaning the Force is in everyone and everything)
2. Creation is sacred (meaning Gaia becomes the face of "God.")
3. "YHWH" (the God of the Old Testament) is "Satan." And Jesus Christ is just "a messiah," not "the messiah."

There will be some slight variations in how this list is expressed but, for the most part, these will be the key points of agreement. Gaia will be present under one or more names: Mary, Sophia, Shekinah, or Shakti/Kali. She will be the bridge between religions and the bridge between "God" and man. As Thomas Schipflinger explains in *Sophia-Maria*:

"Understanding Sophia as the link between the world's religious traditions points to the significance of their relationship. She is the World Soul and the Mother of creation, the source of all Wisdom teachings, the inspiration behind conceptions of the Feminine Divine, and the mediating link to universal salvation through Jesus Christ. She is the Mother, and the world traditions are her children; **She binds them together into one family**..." (371)

One recurring theme that you may notice is the presence of a "fallen," "exiled," or "lost" female spirit (or goddess). In Gnosticism, Sophia "fell" from the Pleroma (or "the fullness"), the spiritual realm where the emanations of "God," known as Aeons dwell. Aeons are incorrectly called angels by Gnostic "Christians".

Figure 18-0-1: Masonic Chart with Code and Prayer published by Humphreys (1846)

Sophia saw the "Father spirit" and desired to create like him (she wanted to be like the "Most High"). In her ambition, she tried to create from herself and she caused herself to fall out of the higher and spiritual realm. Her spirit became the "world soul" (Anima Mundi), also known as Gaia. She is the "fallen" and "lost" light. A similar fate happens to Shekinah in Kabbalistic Judaism, as DeAnne Loper lays out:

"The female Shekinah, now separated from the masculine, descends into exile, destroying the dream of god: '...The very core of reality is G-d's shattered dream, waiting for us to pick up the pieces [of the divine sparks]... it is humankind, not the angels, who can pick it up and reveal it... **That the Infinite Light [Shekinah] is everywhere** is an axiom of the Kabbalah, **held captive within every object**... even within evil itself." (51)

Stephan Hoeller, author of *Gnosticism: A New Light on the Ancient Tradition of Inner Knowing*, explains the role that Sophia played in the garden of Eden:

"...*The Hypostasis of the Archons*, informs us that **not only Eve but also the serpent was inspired and guided by the divine Sophia**. Sophia allowed her wisdom to enter the serpent, who thereby became a teacher and then taught Adam and Eve about their true source. They came to understand that they were not lowly beings created by the Demiurge (in this case, the Creator in the Genesis story), but rather, that their spiritual selves had originated beyond this world, in the fullness of the ultimate Godhead." (28-29)

In *The Hypostasis of the Archons*, Sophia's spirit is in both Eve and the serpent at different times; and not only them but also the tree:

"**The woman of spirit** came to him and spoke with him, saying, 'Rise, Adam.' And when he saw her, he said, 'It is you who have given me life. You will be called 'mother of the living.' For she is my mother. She is the physician, and the woman, and she has given birth... [The princes] said to one another, 'Come, let us sow our seed in her,' and they pursued her. And she laughed at them for their foolishness and blindness. In their clutches **she became a tree**...

Then the female spiritual presence came in the form of the snake, the instructor, and it taught them, saying, 'What did he say to you? Was it,

'From every tree in the garden shall you eat, but from the tree of recognizing evil and good do not eat'?' The woman of flesh [Eve] said, 'Not only did he say 'Don't eat,' but even 'Don't touch it. For the day you eat from it, you will surely die.'' The snake, the instructor, said, 'It is not the case that you will surely die, for out of jealousy he said this to you. Rather, your eyes will open and you will be like gods, recognizing evil and good.' And the female instructing power was taken away from the snake, and she left it behind, merely a thing of the earth."

As I have explained already, the serpent has been a symbol of the goddess from the time when there were no male pagan gods worshiped on the earth. The serpent, as a symbol for Wisdom, is the avatar of the wisdom goddess, Sophia. They are forever intertwined. While there are some differences in narratives, the general Gnostic idea is that Sophia is the mother of the material world. As Stephan A. Hoeller writes of Sophia, after having fallen from the higher realm (the pleroma) among the higher spiritual beings (called Aeons):

"The lower Sophia, Achamoth (an anagram of Chokmah, the Hebrew name for Wisdom), struggles in her alienated condition. She grieves and rages; she sorrows and longs for her original estate. In her distress, she manifests, or emanates, powers that eventually condense into the building blocks of the material universe... She also produces a hybrid form of consciousness, a lion-headed monstrous being who had become the Demiurge [YHWH] (also known as IALDABAOTH, Saclas, and Samael), the 'Artificer" of the created world." (40)

In Gnosticism, Sophia is an emanation of "God." Think of an emanation as a branch of a tree; it's not the tree trunk (God) but it's still the tree. Sophia "falls" and the divinity within her becomes the "divine spark" that is in the material world and, consequently, the "Demiurge" (YHWH) that she gave birth to. While some narratives say that Sophia became the Earth, others say that her son (YHWH) made the earth using Sophia's power that was within him. When her son, the Demiurge, breathed into Adam after forming him in the garden, he inadvertently breathed Sophia's divine spark into him. Sophia, through the serpent, tried to reveal to Adam and Eve their true divine nature. The Demiurge was not happy about that. John Lash, a Gnostic teacher who has a strong disdain for the truth of the Bible, wrote in his book, *Not In His Image*:

"The Demiurge of the Old Testament is an arrogant, demented pretender who claims that humans are 'made in His image.' These four words are the corporate motto of patriarchy. Branded on the human soul, 'Made in His Image' signifies the total enslavement of humanity to an alien, off-planet agenda." (258)

Figure 18-0-2: "Macrocosm and Microcosm" by Tobias Schutz (1654). This shows the goddess as mediator between heaven and earth, God and man, and the infinite and the finite.

Christians, or believers in the Bible, who have already been compromised by unknowingly accepting Gnostic doctrine from wolves in sheep's clothing are in danger of completely falling in line with the unification of the faiths. Gnostic teachers claim that humans were once spiritual beings of light, or angels (to put it in biblical terms), and that our spirits got brought down from heaven by the Demiurge and trapped in the darkness of flesh bodies. But while they say it was "Satan" who did it, the gnostic texts that they are teaching from identify "Satan" as the god of the Bible—Yahawah!

In *Isis Unveiled*, Blavatsky lays out the view of Biblical faith in the mind of a theosophist:

> "The theology of Christendom has been rubbed threadbare by the most serious minds of the day. It is found to be, on the whole, subversive, rather than promotive of spirituality and good morals. Instead of expounding the rules of divine law and justice, it teaches but itself. In place of an ever-living Deity, **it preaches the Evil One, and makes him indistinguishable from God Himself**! 'Lead us not into temptation' is the aspiration of Christians. Who then, is the tempter? Satan? No; the prayer is not addressed to him...it is--the Bible-God of Israel! <u>Our examination of the multitudinous religious faiths that mankind, early and late, have professed, most assuredly indicates that they have all been derived from one primitive source</u>. It would seem as if they were all but different modes of expressing the yearning of the imprisoned human soul for intercourse with supernal spheres." (535)

Aldous Huxley, in *The Perennial Philosophy*, suggests that "the fall" in the garden of Eden was not a violation of God's commandment to not eat from the forbidden tree, but the fall was a passage from the spiritual world into the material world of flesh bodies—falling from the infinite to the finite.

"To be adequate to our experience the [Genesis] myth would have to be modified... it would have to make clear that creation, the incomprehensible passage from the unmanifested One into the manifest multiplicity of nature, from eternity into time, is not merely the prelude and necessary condition of the Fall; to some extent **it is the Fall**." (182)

DeAnne Loper shares the similar Kabbalistic viewpoint on this, reinforcing that a separation from the divine source, or the spiritual world, is the true understanding of the "fall." She says, "In Kabbalah, the sin of Adam is not attributed to his disobedience to God in eating from the tree of knowledge of good and evil, but is the premature separation of the unity of the Sefirot tree." (50)

Elaine Pagels, who wrote *The Gnostic Gospels*, spins the narrative that the early followers of "The Way" (Christians) were in-reality Gnostics. Like the New Agers who would say that Jesus Christ (Yahawashai) was just another teacher or prophet, Elaine says that there can be many Christs:

"Whoever achieves gnosis becomes 'no longer a Christian, but a Christ.' We can see then, that such gnosticism was more than a protest movement against orthodox Christianity. Gnosticism also included a religious perspective that implicitly opposed the development of the kind of institution that became the early catholic church. Those who expected to 'become Christ' themselves were not likely to recognize the institutional structures of the church..." (134)

While I am not a member of the Catholic church, and I am against the institution of it, that doesn't mean I should turn to the opposite extreme and join the Luciferian Gnostics. Jesus Christ warned us about these types of deceivers:

"And as he sat upon the mount of Olives, the disciples came unto him privately, saying, Tell us, when shall these things be? and what shall be the sign of thy coming, and of the end of the world? And Jesus answered and said unto them, Take heed that no man deceive you. **For many shall come in my name, saying, I am Christ; and shall deceive many**." (Matthew 24:3-4)

Another common ground with these many religions is that they aim to unite all of humanity. Only the true Biblical God of Abraham, Isaac, and Jacob calls for His children (Israelite and gentile) to come out from the rest of the world and be separate. The world's mantra is, "We're all connected." Led Zeppelin plays their instruments like the Pied Piper, crying, "All is one. One is all!" In their song, "Stairway to Heaven," they sing of "a lady we all know who shines white light and wants to show that everything still turns to gold."

That lady is Lucifer. She is the Alma Mater (Virgin Mother). She's the "girl with the sun in her eyes" that the Beatles sang about in their song, "Lucy in the Sky with Diamonds." You can find this lawless woman Lucy in Hollywood, where they sell Kali fornication. The mystery religion (the goddess religion) that was driven underground has been revitalized in the New Age and Gnostic doctrines that are being spread in books, through online teachers, and pushed by Hollywood and the entertainment industry. Because we have not been taught who Lucifer **truly** is, she has been able to operate with little resistance. But we should have known— who is as subtle as a serpent but a woman? It's not about strength, as Proverbs 7:26-27 tells us: "For she hath cast down many wounded: yea, **many strong men have been slain by her**."

No, I am not saying that women in general are evil. Please, don't take the wrong message away from this book. I am only pointing out that women, by their nature, are more like the serpent. *Merriam-Webster* defines **subtle** as, "delicate, elusive," and "difficult to understand or perceive." As the Bible warns us of the STRANGE WOMAN, "her ways are moveable, **that thou canst not know them**." (Proverbs 5:6) The HARLOT is "**subtil** of heart". (Proverbs 7:10) The entertainment industry, through the divas (the High Priestesses) as a host body, are literally performing rituals in which Mystery Babylon is being worshiped. This is what the Scarlet Woman or Lady in Red really comes down to. The diva (meaning GODDESS) embodies Lucifer on Earth; worshiping her leads you to becoming drunken by the spirit of whoredoms.

Figure 18-0-3: "Lilith" by Kenyon Cox (1891).

CHAPTER 19: KING OF KINGS, LORD OF LORDS

"And I saw heaven opened, and behold a white horse; and he that sat upon him was called Faithful and True, and in righteousness he doth judge and make war. His eyes were as a flame of fire, and on his head were many crowns; and he had a name written, that no man knew, but he himself. And he was clothed with a vesture dipped in blood: and his name is called **The Word of God**. And the armies which were in heaven followed him upon white horses, clothed in fine linen, white and clean. And out of his mouth goeth a sharp sword, that with it he should smite the nations: and he shall rule them with a rod of iron: and he treadeth the winepress of the fierceness and wrath of Almighty God. And he hath on his vesture and on his thigh a name written, **KING OF KINGS, AND LORD OF LORDS**." (Revelation 19:11-16)

I praise my Father in Heaven for allowing me to know Him and His son, Jesus Christ. Over ten years ago, I was well on my way to unknowingly embracing the goddess religion. Even though I grew up going to church I became agnostic when I reached my 20s. I joined the Navy in my last year of high school and shipped off only six days after I graduated. I got to travel the world, and during my travels I saw the other religions that existed with my own eyes. During those times, especially when I was stationed in Japan, I thought, "They can't all be wrong. Maybe God reveals himself to different people in different forms." Nobody had to tell me that. I didn't read it in a book. My mind automatically went there on its own. I would have easily ended up worshiping at the altar of Mother Nature, had the Most High turned me over to a reprobate mind.

Praise be to Yah Almighty, because He didn't let me go. He kept me through my foolishness, even when I rolled my car while speeding and could have died while my wife was pregnant with our first child. He was merciful to me! I was awakened from my "sleep" by the Most High in 2013, when I came across YouTube videos showing how close we were to the return of Jesus Christ. Those videos shook me awake. I repented for my wickedness and turned my heart back to Him. I distinctly remember saying to my Father in Heaven, "**I made a big mistake**." He began a work in me back then that is continuing today. Day by day, I am being conformed to the glorious image of His son, Jesus Christ.

My journey towards writing this book began, if I remember correctly, in 2014. That's when I asked my Father Yahawah in Heaven to help me understand the book of Revelation because I was confused about the timing of the gathering to Christ (what most know of as the "rapture"). Around that time, I also began to question if the Jezebel spirit was a real thing and if it was in the Bible; I believed that if it was real, it would be there. I asked Yah to guide me as I began studying the Bible to find the truth; I had no clue I would end up here right now writing a book to tell the world that the Jezebel spirit is Lucifer, and that Lucifer is—in truth—a female spirit.

Figure 19-0-1: Column of the Immaculate Conception, Rome.

What I thought I saw back then (by that time in early 2015) was unsettling and I didn't really want to just come out and tell people about it. But I was told by the pastor of a church that I was attending at the time that the Most High gave him a word for me. There were two things, he said: I was told to pray for my sister, and I was told that I should "stop sitting on" what I had, to paraphrase a little because I don't remember the exact words. I didn't know if I believed he was right or not, but I kept the words in my heart. Not long after that, I was informed that my grandmother who raised me went into hospice. I traveled across the country to see her, with my sister, and we got to see our grandmother one last time and tell her that we loved her before she passed away.

When I returned home, I thought about what I was told. I just remember thinking, "Okay, I'm going to do this. I'm going to start telling people." I couldn't think of anything else that the pastor's words could have been about. I uploaded my first video about the Queen of Heaven in the summer of 2015. After that, I started a YouTube channel that would be dedicated to this subject called *Daylight Riders*. About a year or so after that, I started a second one called *Babylon Watch*. For the next eight years, I was seeking the truth and praying to the Most High with fear and trembling. I can't count the number of times I have pleaded with Him that He would remove far from me vanity and lies and lead me into all truth by his Holy Spirit.

I have seen so much over the years that has left me dumbfounded. I've often asked, "How can it be that no one else has seen this?" It's far more than I could put into a book. In fact, I'm still rediscovering things that I once knew but forgot because there was so much out there. In Nashville, Tennessee, there stands a reconstruction of the Parthenon from Athens, Greece. When I first saw pictures of the 42-foot tall (12.8 meter) statue of Athena inside it, I thought to myself, "Hey, where is all the outrage from Christians?" Why did no one tell me about it? Why did I have to discover it on my own?

But then, why was I surprised? The Statue of Libertas has been standing in New York Harbor for over a century. The goddess is on the back of our money. She's on top of the Capitol Building. She's outside the courthouses with a blindfold and a pair of scales. Babylon has so swamped us with so much goddess imagery that we don't even register it anymore.

There were many times when I didn't want to see and know anything about this and I wanted to run away. Did I have doubts? ABSOLUTELY. When I said I was in **fear and trembling**, I meant it. I'm a man who barely got passing grades in high school and then I dropped out of community college after wasting the money I got for college from the Navy. Who was I to challenge what the Bible scholars taught about Lucifer for centuries, if not longer? I mean it when I tell you that there were times when I wished that I had never even looked into this matter. But despite those difficult inner struggles, I'm here on this day and I know what I know. I never imagined I would be writing a book about anything with my level of education. To the Most High God Yahawah be praise and glory for helping me to do it.

My prayer is that I have been faithful with what Yah has given me. At the end of the day, that is all that matters. I ask that you take everything that I have presented in this book to the Most High in prayer. Let Yah be true and every man a liar. Thank you for taking the time to read this book. I pray that it will be a blessing to you. To those who do the will of our Father in Heaven, may the grace of our Lord and Savior Jesus Christ (Yahawashai) be with you!

ACKNOWLEDGMENTS

First, I want to thank the subscribers to my YouTube channels; your support over the years was needed and every comment that you left on my videos made a difference. While my channels *Daylight Riders* and *Babylon Watch* are both around 6k subscribers, due to the mysterious workings of YouTube, my reach always seemed very limited. It was good to receive words of encouragement when they came.

Second, I would like to acknowledge the following content creators who do great work in exposing and reproving the unfruitful works of darkness. It probably goes without saying but we don't agree on every issue; despite those differences, however, I encourage you to view their content and subscribe to their channels:

MYSTERY OF INIQUITY EXPOSED (on Odysee.com).

World Wide Widow (on YouTube.com).

DON'T JUST BE ANOTHER BRICK IN THE WALL 2 (on YouTube.com).

ExposingConspiracy (on Rumble.com).

Shaking My Head Productions (on YouTube).

Pastor Michael Hoggard (on YouTube).

BIBLIOGRAPHY

"About Saint Lucy." https://www.stlucy-campbell.org/about-staint-lucy/. *St. Lucy Catholic Parish*. Accessed 10 December 2023

"Ankh." https://www.newworldencyclopedia.org/entry/Ankh. *New World Encyclopedia* Accessed 04 December 2023

"Paleo-Hebrew alphabet." https://en.wikipedia.org/wiki/Paleo-Hebrew_alphabet. *Wikipedia*. Accessed   18 January 2023

Begg, Ean. *The Cult of the Black Virgin*. 1985. Wilmette: Chiron Publications, 1996.

Best, Stewart. "Why America is Babylon" https://rumble.com/v1x484k-why-america-is-babylon-stewart-best.html. 1996

Blavatksy, Helena P. *Isis Unveiled*. Vol. 2. 1877. Orlando: Pantianos Classics, 2023. 2 vols.
---. *The Secret Doctrine. Vol. 1*. 1888. London: Theosophical University Press, 2022. 2 vols.

Børns. "Electric Love." *Dopamine*, Interscope, 2014. https://youtu.be/RYr96YYEaZY?si=GmKl1U_NyM6WVBtG

Bradford, Brian, Dr. *Arabian Religion Before Muhammad*. Middletown: Brian Bradford, 2014.

Brooks, Meredith. "Bitch." *Blurring the Edges,* City Lab Sound Design, 1997.

Brueton, Diana. *Many Moons*. New York: Prentice Hall Press, 1991.

Burns, Cathy, Dr. *Hidden Secrets of the Eastern Star*. 1994. Mt. Carmel: Sharing, 2006.
---. *Masonic and Occult Symbols Illustrated*. 1998. Mt. Carmel: Sharing, 2013.

Butler, Alan and Janet Wolter. *America Nation of the Goddess: The Venus Families and the Founding of   the United States*. Rochester: Destiny Books, 2015.

Butler, Alan. *City of the Goddess: Freemasons, the Sacred Feminine, and the Secret Beneath The Seat of Power in Washington, DC*. London: Watkins Publishing, 2011.
---. *The Goddess, The Grail & The Lodge*. Winchester: O Books, 2004.

Cohen, Abraham. *Everyman's Talmud: The Major Teachings of Rabbinic Sages*. 1949. New York: Schocken Books, Inc., 1975.

"Collection of the Sumerian Temple Hymns."
https://www.angelfire.com/tx/tintirbabylon/INANNA.html.
  Babylon Magick. Accessed 24 November 2023

Day, John. *Yahweh and the Gods and Goddesses of Canaan*. London: Sheffield Academic Press, 2000.

Delta Spirit. "California." *Delta Spirit,* Rounder Records, 2012.

d'Este, Sorita and David Rankine. *The Cosmic Shekinah: A Historical Study of the Goddess of the Old Testament and Kabbalah*. London: Avalonia, 2011

Fortune, Dion. *The Mystical Qabalah*. 1935. San Francisco: Red Wheel/Wieser, 2000.

Foubister, Linda. *Goddess In The Grass: Serpentine Mythology and the Great Goddess*. Toronto: Linda Foubister, 2003.

Frazer, James G. *The Golden Bough*. 1981. Avenel: Gramercy Books, 1993.

Freke, Timothy and Peter Gandy. *Jesus and the Lost Goddess*. New York: Three Rivers Press, 2001.

Frymer-Kensky, Tiva. *In the Wake of the Goddesses*. New York: The Free Press, 1992.

George, Demetra and Douglas Bloch. *Asteroid Goddesses*. 1986. Lake Worth: Ibis Press, 2003.

Genesis, Tommy. "God is Wild (Film)." MMXVIII Downtown Records, 2018.
https://youtu.be/wyYQQzgAX00?si=rgG1bXChi6FXfg7i

"Goddess as Queen Bee - Artemis of Ephesus."
https://www.floweringmoon.com/blogs/news/goddess-as-queen-bee-artemis-of-ephesus?_pos=1&_sid=0bcf8c434&_ss=r. *Flowering Moon*. Accessed 30 November 2023

Hall, Manly P. *The Lost Keys of Freemasonry*. New York: Penguin Group, 2006
--- . *The Secret Teachings of All Ages*. 1928. New York: Penguin Group, 2003

Harris, Jonathan. *Constantinople: Capital of Byzantium*. 2007. London: Bloomsbury, 2017.

Hislop, Alexander. *The Two Babylons*. 1903. Lexington: Forgotten Books, 2012.

162

Hodder, Ian, ed. *Religion in the Emergence of Civilization: Catalhoyuk as a Case Study*. Cambridge: Cambridge University Press, 2010.

Hoeller, Stephan A. *Gnosticism: New Light on the Ancient Tradition of Inner Knowing*. Wheaton: Quest Books, 2002.

Holy Bible: King James Version.

Huxley, Aldous. *The Perennial Philosophy*. 1944. New York: HarperCollins Publishers, 2009.

Kien, Jenny. *Reinstating the Divine Woman in Judaism*. Florida: Universal Publishers, 2000

Kollerstrom, Nick. "The Metal-Planet Affinities - The Sevenfold Pattern." https://www.alchemywebsite.com/kollerstrom_sevenfold.html. *Practical Alchemy*. Accessed 09 December 2023

Lash, John Lamb. *Not In His Image*. White River Junction: Chelsea Green Publishing, 2006.

Led Zeppelin. "Stairway to Heaven." *Led Zeppelin IV*, Atlantic Records, 1971.

"Liberty Enlightening the World." https://www.nps.gov/stli/index.htm. *National Park Service*. Accessed 09 December 2023

Loper, DeAnne. *Kabbalah Secrets Christians Need to Know*. Monee: DeAnne Loper, 2019.

Lucy Trent, Alice. *The Feminine Universe*. The Golden Order Press, 1997.

Macoy, Robert. *A Dictionary of Freemasonry*. 1989. New York: Gramercy Books, 2000.

"Madonna." https://www.etymonline.com/word/madonna. *Online Etymology Dictionary*. Accessed 26 November 2023

Matthews, Caitlin. *Sophia: Goddess of Wisdom, Bride of God*. Wheaton: Quest Books, 2001.

National Geographic Society. *Mysteries of the Ancient World*. National Geographic Society, 1979.

"Nineveh." https://www.worldhistory.org/nineveh. *World History Encyclopedia*. Accessed 24 November 2023

Pagels, Elaine. *The Gnostic Gospels*. 1979. New York: Vintage Books, 1989.

Patai, Raphael. *The Hebrew Goddess*. 1967. Detroit: Wayne State University Press, 1990.

"Persephone." https://www.theoi.com/Khthonios/Persephone.html. *THEOI GREEK MYTHOLOGY*. Accessed 03 December 2023

Peters, Francis E. *Mecca: A Literary History of the Muslim Holy Land*. Princeton: Princeton University Press, 1994.

Rodgers, John, Dr. *New Age Bible—Hidden Truth Revealed*. New Brunswick: Inner Light Publications, 1992.

Schipflinger, Thomas. *Sophia-Maria: A Holistic View of Creation*. York Beach: Samuel Weiser, Inc, 1998.

"Semiramis." https://www.worldhistory.org/Semiramis/. *World History Encyclopedia*. Accessed 26 November 2023

Silva, Freddy. *The Lost Art of Resurrection: Initiation, Secret Chambers, and the Quest for the Otherworld*. 2014. Rochester: Invisible Temple, 2017.

Sjoo, Monica and Barbara Mor. *The Great Cosmic Mother: Rediscovering the Religion of the Earth*. 1987. New York: HarperOne, 1991.

Stavish, Mark. *Freemasonry: Rituals, Symbols & History of the Secret Society*. Woodbury: Llewellyn, 2007.

Soundgarden. "Black Hole Sun." *Superunknown*, A&M, 1994.

"Strong's Concordance." https://www.blueletterBible.org/. *Blue Letter Bible*. Accessed 11 December 2023

Stone, Merlin. *When God was a Woman*. Great Britain: Virago Limited, 1976.
---. *Ancient Mirrors of Womanhood*. 1979. Boston: Beacon Press, 1990.

"Subtle," https://www.merriam-webster.com/dictionary/subtle. *Merriam-Webster*. Accessed 10 December 2023

Tetlow, Jim, Roger Oakland, Brad Myers. *Queen of Rome, Queen of Islam, Queen of All*. Fairport: Eternal Productions, 2006.

164

The Beatles. "Lucy in the Sky with Diamonds." *Sgt. Pepper's Lonely Hearts Club Band*, Parlophone Records, 1967.

"The Exaltation of Inanna." https://www.angelfire.com/tx/tintirbabylon/INANNA.html. *Babylon Magick*. Accessed 24 November 2023

"The Exaltation of Inanna." https://babylonian-collection.yale.edu/sites/default/files/files/Hallo_Van%20Dijk%20(1968)%20-%20Exaltation%20of%20Inanna_YNER%203.pdf. *Yale University*. Accessed 24 November 2023

"The Higgs Boson." https://home.web.cern.ch/science/physics/higgs-boson. *CERN*. Accessed 22 November 2023

"The Ishtar Gate and the Deities of Babylon." https://www.ancient-origins.net/ancient-places-asia/ishtar-gate-and-deities-babylon-001868. *Ancient Origins*. Accessed 24 November 2023

The Seal of Liberty author. "Sigil of Lucifer - Scottish Rite's symbol of liberty." https://youtu.be/VhxJBUDZv2Y?si=0ul7o0YkfERAyc21.

"The Story Behind Columbia Pictures' Iconic Logo: How Photographer Found Model for 1992 Shoot." https://people.com/the-story-behind-columbia-pictures-iconic-logo-how-photographer-found-the-model-for-1992-shoot-7506092. *People*. Accessed 16 December 2023

"The Temple Hymns: translation." https://etcsl.orinst.ox.ac.uk/section4/tr4801.htm. *The Electronic Text Corpus of Sumerian Literature*. Accessed 25 November 2023

"The Ten Principles of the Georgia Guidestones, America's Strangest Monument." https://pioneerproductions.blogspot.com/2020/07/the-ten-principles-of-georgia.html. *Ennyman's Territory*. Accessed 30 November 2023

"The Hypostasis of the Archons, Nag Hammadi Codex II, 4." http://www.gnosis.org/naghamm/Hypostas-Barnstone.html. *The Gnostic Society Library*. Accessed 03 December 2023

"The Veil of Isis." https://isiopolis.com/2023/07/09/the-veil-of-isis/. *Isiopolis*. Accessed 02 December 2023

Trainor, Meghan. "Mother." *Takin' It Back*, Epic, 2023. https://youtu.be/9coyY-SPIXU?si=9Nd3M5EuYpvQCanP

Walker, Barbara G. *The Woman's Dictionary of Symbols and Sacred Objects*. New York: HarperOne, 1988.

---. The Women's Encyclopedia of Myths and Secrets. New York: HarperOne, 1983.

Ward, John Sebastian Marlow. *The Sign Language of the Mysteries*. 1928. Whitefish: Kessinger Legacy Reprints, 2010. 2 vols.

"Yoni." https://www.britannica.com/topic/yoni. *Britannica*. Accessed 30 November 2023

IMAGE LINKS

Alma Mater statue by Daniel Chester French, 1903, Columbia University, New York City - https://en.wikipedia.org/wiki/File:Columbia_University,_NYC_(June_2014)_-_09.JPG

Anima Mundi - https://commons.wikimedia.org/wiki/File:Anima_Mundi_(by_Robert_Fludd,_Utriusque_Cosmi_Historia,_1617).png

Astrological sign Virgo at the Wisconsin State Capitol - https://commons.wikimedia.org/wiki/File:Astrological_sign_Virgo_at_the_Wisconsin_State_Capitol.jpg

Attis - https://hellenicfaith.com/attis/

Auspice Maria banner - https://www.youtube.com/live/vrRvpZ2hxFE?si=57qRhROthX54NdfS

Auspice Maria engraving - https://www.catholiccompany.com/getfed/what-is-the-auspice-maria/

Beauty from Beaumont's Beauty and the Beast (1756) - https://www.pookpress.co.uk/beaumont-beauty-beast/

Britnnia - https://commons.wikimedia.org/wiki/File:Britannia-Statue.jpg

CBS logo - https://www.freep.com/story/entertainment/television/2021/12/14/cbs-news-detroit-streaming-tv-newscasts/6506166001/

Columbia Pictures Logo - https://en.m.wikipedia.org/wiki/File:Columbia_Pictures_logo.png

Column of the Immaculate Conception, Rome - https://en.wikipedia.org/wiki/File:Immacolatacolonnaroma.JPG

Coronation of the Virgin - https://en.wikipedia.org/wiki/File:Diego_Vel%C3%A1zquez_-_Coronation_of_the_Virgin_-_Prado.jpg

Dos Equis logo - https://otbsd.com/dos-equis/
"Fall of Man." https://en.wikipedia.org/wiki/Fall_of_man

First Degree Tracing Board Josiah Bowring - https://artuk.org/discover/artworks/first-degree-tracing-board-192138

Freemasonry instructing the people - https://www.meisterdrucke.fr/fine-art-prints/Charles-Mercereau/188435/La-franc-ma%C3%A7onnerie-instruisant-le-peuple%2C-1875.html

General Manual of Freemasonry - https://450.fm/2023/08/27/manuel-general-de-la-franc-maconnerie/

Giovanni Battista Tiepolo's Immaculate Conception - https://upload.wikimedia.org/wikipedia/commons/thumb/0/03/The_Immaculate_Conception%2C_by_Giovanni_Battista_Tiepolo%2C_from_Prado_in_Google_Earth.jpg/1114px-

The_Immaculate_Conception%2C_by_Giovanni_Battista_Tiepolo%2C_from_Prado_in_Google_Earth.jpg

Goddess and serpent in Eden - https://www.ancient-origins.net/sites/default/files/ada-and-eve.jpg

Guanyin - http://en.people.cn/n3/2019/0323/c90000-9559614-3.html

"Hamsa Hand" - https://commons.wikimedia.org/wiki/File:WPVA-khamsa.svg

Horus on Isis's lap - https://commons.wikimedia.org/wiki/File:Isis_Suckling_Horus_%281878%29_-_TIMEA.jpg#file

Ishtar gate - https://en.wikipedia.org/wiki/File:Pergamonmuseum_Ishtartor_05.jpg

Isis covering Osiris - https://en.m.wikipedia.org/wiki/File:Philae_Temple_Egypt_Goddess_Isis_As_Angel_Mural_Artwork_2004-10-11.jpg (Kim Bach)

Isis covering Osiris - https://isiopolis.com/2019/01/26/why-does-isis-have-wings-2/

Isis knot - https://commons.wikimedia.org/wiki/File:Tit_(Isis_knot)_amulet_MET_DP109370.jpg

Isis with spread wings - https://www.femigod.com/goddess-isis-3-invocations-for-magical-manifesting/

Kali - https://in.pinterest.com/pin/613545149214509650/

Kali on Empire State building -
https://x.com/ShimaliP/status/630616053568008192?s=20

"Kiss of Venus" -
https://en.m.wikipedia.org/wiki/File:Venus_geocentric_orbit_curve_simplified_Line_%2
8pentagram%29.svg

Libery coins - https://libertycoin.com/2023-american-silver-eagle-1-oz-1-bu-23-ase-bu/
        --- https://www.apmex.com/product/271800/2023-1-oz-gold-eagle-bu-
coin?feed=gmc&utm_campaign=&utm_content=271800-
pla&utm_source=google&utm_medium=cpc&utm_campaign=&utm_content=&gad_sou
rce=1&gclid=CjwKCAiAvdCrBhBREiwAX6-
6UuI0PT5K0QTxSSHkrXBJjpkjfJvq3lS6pGjne9zljawHaRMYqBjRmxoCB7QQAvD_BwE
        --- https://www.usmint.gov/coins/coin-medal-programs/american-liberty/2015-
high-relief-gold-coin

Lilith by Kenyon Cox - https://pixels.com/featured/cox-lilith-1891-granger.html

Lust tarot card - https://wildlyfreewoman.net/tag/tarot-cards/

Macrocosm and Microcosm -
https://commons.wikimedia.org/wiki/File:Harmonia_macrocosmi_cum_microcosmi.jpg

Masonic apron - https://bricksmasons.com/products/master-mason-blue-lodge-apron-
royal-blue-radiant-square-compass-
g?variant=39803810087030&currency=USD&cmp_id=17332500407&adg_id=&kwd=&d
evice=c&gad_source=1&gclid=CjwKCAiAvdCrBhBREiwAX6-
6Uhg7EWZVVVNnp3v0mNiybw6Uuw2OruKhsljQ33ZoHPP9uSycYliUyxoCHOIQAvD_BwE

Masonic beehive drawing - https://peakd.com/symbols/@cardinalkpatrick/the-sacred-
bee-and-what-it-means-to-the-holy-grail-royalty

Masonic Chart with Code and Prayer published by Humphreys in 1846 -
https://bricksmasons.com/products/masonic-chart-with-code-and-prayer-1800s-
americana-1-piece-canvas

Masonic Esotericism 1st third of 19th century Engraving -
https://gnosticstudies.org/index.php/the-mysteries/the-mystery-religions-of-the-
ancients-part-4/

Masonic Register 1876 - https://en.wikipedia.org/wiki/File:Masonic_Register_1876.jpg

Mastercard logo - https://en.m.wikipedia.org/wiki/File:MasterCard_Logo.svg

Mother Svea - https://commons.wikimedia.org/wiki/File:Sveahuset_i_G%C3%B6teborg_-_takstaty.jpg

Mother of God at Hagia Sophia - https://www.worldhistory.org/image/7973/the-virgin-and-child-mosaic-hagia-sophia/

Okay hand sign - https://en.wikipedia.org/wiki/File:LG_WHISEN_%EC%86%90%EC%97%B0%EC%9E%AC_%EC%A7%80%EB%A9%B4_%EA%B4%91%EA%B3%A0_%EC%B4%AC%EC%98%81_%EC%82%AC%EC%A7%84_(30)_hand_only.jpg

Pentagram of Venus - https://www.eso.org/public/outreach/eduoff/vt-2004/Education/edu1app5.html

Pieta de Michelangelo - https://commons.wikimedia.org/wiki/File:Pieta_de_Michelangelo_-_Vaticano.jpg

Platonic solid - https://commons.wikimedia.org/wiki/File:Kepler_Hexahedron_Earth.jpg

Pyramid on dollar - https://www.rd.com/list/dollar-bill-symbols/

Roma coin - https://www.raptureofchurch.com/Revelation/10BabylontheGreat.htm

Rose - https://commons.wikimedia.org/wiki/File:Rosa_Precious_platinum.jpg

Salt Lake Mormon Temple doorknob - https://en.m.wikipedia.org/wiki/File:SL_Temple_doornob.jpg

Satelite images of Washington D.C. where screenshot from Google Maps.

Sculpture of Weeping Woman by Nikolaus Geiger - https://www.facebook.com/MDuMarie/photos/a.408261212547595/3583159545057730/?type=3

Seated woman of Catalhoyuk - https://commons.wikimedia.org/wiki/File:%C3%87atalh%C3%B6y%C3%BCk_oturan_ilah%C9%99_fiqurunun_%C3%B6nd%C9%99n_g%C3%B6r%C3%BCn%C3%BC%C5%9F%C3%BC.jpg

Secret Figures of the Rosicrucians 1785. - https://commons.wikimedia.org/wiki/File:SophiaMystical.jpg

Sigil of Lucifer - https://commons.wikimedia.org/wiki/File:Sigil_of_Lucifer.svg

Sign of the horns - https://commons.wikimedia.org/wiki/File:Mano_cornuta.jpg

Sopdet - https://en.wikipedia.org/wiki/Sopdet#/media/File:Sopdet.svg

Spiral goddess - https://commons.wikimedia.org/wiki/File:Spiral_Goddess_symbol_neo-pagan.svg

Square - https://commons.wikimedia.org/wiki/File:Regular_polygon_4_annotated.svg

Square and compass - https://www.masonicexchange.com/Simple-Square-Compass-with-G-Masonic-Vinyl-Decal_p_1634.html

Statue of freedom - https://en.wikipedia.org/wiki/Statue_of_Freedom#/media/File:Statue_of_Freedom,_Washington,_D.C.jpg

Statue of Liberty Enlightening the World - https://commons.wikimedia.org/wiki/File:Lady_Liberty_under_a_blue_sky_(cropped).jpg

St. Lucy procession - (Claudia Gründer) https://upload.wikimedia.org/wikipedia/commons/archive/0/04/20091207123253%21Lucia-13.12.06.jpg

Stone honeycomb carving in Ephesus by Mucahitgul - https://pixabay.com/photos/architectural-pattern-moti-2407725/

The Black Stone - https://commons.wikimedia.org/wiki/File:The_Blackstone.jpg

The Blazing Star - https://www.thesquaremagazine.com/mag/article/202305the-blazing-star/

The Bohemian Club logo - https://en.wikipedia.org/wiki/File:Bohemian_Club_logo.png

The Chalice (Holy Grail) - https://images.musicasacra.com/photos/index.php?/category/1

The Damsel of the Sanct Grael - https://commons.wikimedia.org/wiki/File:Dante_Gabriel_Rossetti_-_The_Damsel_of_the_Sanct_Grael_(1874).jpg

The Fall by Kenyon Cox -
https://upload.wikimedia.org/wikipedia/commons/9/9f/Kenyon_Cox_-
_The_Fall_%281892%29.jpg

The goddess and the serpent - https://www.ancient-origins.net/myths-legends/lilith-
ancient-demon-dark-deity-or-sex-goddess-005908

The Lady of all Nations -
https://commons.wikimedia.org/wiki/File:The_Lady_of_All_Nations_Image.jpg

Universal dictionary of arts, sciences, and literature. London -
https://biblio.ie/book/reproduccin-reproduction-49757551122-encyclopaedia-
londinensis-universal/d/1454887679

Venus and dove - https://www.cointalk.com/threads/venus-and-doves.361132/

Veiled Isis - https://commons.wikimedia.org/wiki/File:Auguste_Puttemans_Isis_2.jpg

Venus (Lucifer) standing on lions - https://www.thecollector.com/who-was-the-goddess-
ishtar-inanna/

Venus von Willendorf -
https://commons.wikimedia.org/wiki/File:Venus_von_Willendorf_01.jpg

Venus of Arles by François Girardon -
https://commons.wikimedia.org/wiki/File:Venus_of_Arles_Louvre_Ma439_n01.jpg

Venus with apple - https://en.m.wikipedia.org/wiki/File:Bertel_Thorvaldsen_-
_Venus_with_Apple.JPG

Virgin in the parish church of St. Ulrich in Gröden - Ortisei Val Gardena Italy -
https://commons.wikimedia.org/wiki/File:Lusenberg-Virgin.jpg

Virgo - https://en.wikipedia.org/wiki/File:Sidney_Hall_-_Urania%27s_Mirror_-_Virgo.jpg

Virgo symbol - https://en.wikipedia.org/wiki/File:Virgo_symbol_(bold).svg
Widow weeping over a pillar - https://www.universalfreemasonry.org/en/article/the-
broken-column

www.ingramcontent.com/pod-product-compliance
Lightning Source LLC
Chambersburg PA
CBHW060523130626
46553CB00002B/627